D0940812

ROYAL BRITISH COLU.

HANDBOOK

Food Plants
OF COASTAL FIRST PEOPLES

NANCY J. TURNER

UBC PRESS / VANCOUVER

Published by UBC Press in collaboration with the Royal British Columbia Museum.

This edition was edited, designed and typeset by Gerry Truscott, RBCM. Set entirely in Baskerville (body text: 10/12).

The front cover photograph and most of the inside photographs are by R.D. and N.J. Turner. © R.D. and N.J. Turner. Copyright information and credits for the other photographs are on page 164, which is an extension of the copyright page.

Printed in Canada.

Canadian Cataloguing in Publication Data
Turner, Nancy J., 1947-
    Food plants of coastal First Peoples

    Co-published by the Royal British Columbia Museum.
    First published as: Food Plants of British Columbia Indians. Pt. 1. Coastal Peoples. British Columbia Provincial Museum, 1975. (Handbook no. 34)
    Includes bibliographical references: pp. 151-58.
    ISBN 0-7748-0533-1

    1. Indians of North America - British Columbia - Pacific Coast - Food. 2. Ethnobotany - British Columbia - Pacific Coast. 3. Wild Plants, Edible - British Columbia - Pacific Coast. 4. Indians of North America - Ethnobotany - British Columbia - Pacific Coast. I. Royal British Columbia Museum. II Title. III Title: Food Plants of British Columbia Indians.

E78.C3T87 1995   581.6'32'089970711   C95-960424-3

UBC Press
University of British Columbia
6344 Memorial Road
Vancouver, B.C. V6T 1Z2
(604) 822-3259
Fax: 1-800-668-0821
E-mail: orders@ubcpress.ubc.ca

Royal British Columbia Museum
675 Belleville Street
Victoria, B.C. V8V 1X4
Attention: Publishing Services

CONTENTS

Foreword   v

Preface to the First Edition (1975)   vii

Preface to the Second Edition   ix

Introduction   1

    Format   3

    Sources of Information   3

    The Physical Environment   4

    First Peoples of the Coast   7

    Plants in the Diet of First Peoples   9

    Harvesting Food Plants   11

    Preparation of Food Plants   13

    Food Plants Throughout the Seasons   15

    Food Plants and Etiquette   17

    Trading Food Plants   17

Seaweeds   19

Ferns and Their Relatives   23

Conifers   32

Flowering Plants: Monocotyledons   36

Flowering Plants: Dicotyledons   55

Appendix 1: Some Non-native Food Plants
    Used by Coastal First Peoples   133

Appendix 2: Some Plants Considered to Be
    Poisonous or Inedible by Coastal First
    Peoples   138

Glossary   146

References (1975)   151

Additional References   155

Index   159

FOREWORD

The traditional diet of the aboriginal people occupying the northwest coast of North America was predominantly fish, shellfish and sea mammals. Nevertheless, coastal First Peoples had an intimate knowledge of local flora, recognizing and using more than 200 species of plants for food, medicine and other purposes. Few if any plants could be described as being a staple food, but as both aboriginal myths and anthropological descriptions indicate, at certain times plants were an important supplement to native diet.

A popular image prevails that there was an abundance of food on the northwest coast. A close analysis of the situation indicates that at times, especially in local areas, starvation threatened. In early spring, roots, bulbs and shoots were of special importance; they relieved the monotony of the winter's fare and at times provided practically the only source of food. Other plant parts, fruits especially, were regular constituents of native diet, but again it must be emphasized that these were not staples.

Ethnographic descriptions of the gathering, preserving and preparation of edible plants by coastal First Peoples exist, but generally these descriptions are limited to obscure anthropological journals, not readily available to the public. It is, therefore, appropriate that the Royal British Columbia Museum provide this information in an easy-to-use and accessible format.

In preparing this handbook on the use of edible plants by the aboriginal people of the British Columbia coast, Dr Nancy Turner has skilfully and intelligibly presented material from existing publications and, more importantly, has added new information she has gathered. While many aspects of the traditional culture of coastal First Peoples remain strong and viable today, there are few people alive who retain detailed knowledge of traditional plant usage. These people have assisted Dr Turner in presenting the most detailed ethnobotanical studies relating to British Columbia First Peoples to date. Her extensive research has been published elsewhere in scientific journals and monographs, and it is indeed welcome that she is now sharing her knowledge in this popular form.

Peter L. Macnair
Curator of Ethnology
British Columbia Provincial Museum
1975

PREFACE TO THE FIRST EDITION

In the past three decades or so there has been a growing interest of continental proportion in both outdoor survival and native cultures. The study of edible wild plants used by First Peoples is a natural topic to consider when these two interests are combined.

My own fascination with the subject of First Peoples' plant foods extends over more than fifteen years, during which time I subjected first my parents and later my husband to innumerable concoctions and samples of wild menu, only some of which they felt deserved the term "food". Members of my family still shudder at my first attempts to make "Indian ice-cream" from Soapberries, or at the gummy results of my culinary experiments with Blue Camas bulbs. Other adventures in native cuisine were more favourably received, and some wild food products, such as wild onions and Labrador Tea, have since become household commodities for us.

In the course of the last six years, mainly in conjunction with my university studies, I have had the privilege of learning about the use of wild plants in native cultures from many extremely knowledgeable and enthusiastic aboriginal people in several different parts of the province. My sincere appreciation goes to all of them, especially to Florence Davidson, and Emma and William Matthews of Massett; George Young; Maude Moody; Agnes Moody; Solomon and Emma Wilson, and Becky Pearson of Skidegate; Margaret Siwallace, David Moody and Felicity Walkus of Bella Coola; Cecelia August of Sechelt; Dominic Charlie, Andy Natural and Louis Miranda of North Vancouver; Christopher Paul of the Tsartlip Reserve, Brentwood Bay; Richard and Maude Harry of the East Saanich Reserve; Lucy Brown and Agnes Cranmer of Alert Bay; and Bob Wilson and Mr and Mrs Tom Johnson of Fort Rupert. Without these people, this book would not have been possible. I would like to dedicate it to them.

I would also like to thank R. Bouchard and Dorothy Kennedy of the B.C. Indian Language Project, Victoria, for permission to include information on edible plants of the Mainland Comox people, which they recorded from Rose Mitchell, Bill Mitchell, John Mitchell and Jeannie Dominick, all of Squirrel Cove near Powell River. Ms Kennedy also provided the account of collecting hemlock cambium by the Nuxalk, which she obtained from Margaret Siwallace.

I am indebted to my two university research advisers, Dr M.A.M. Bell, Department of Biology, University of Victoria, and Dr Roy L. Taylor, Director of the Botanical Garden, University of British Columbia, for encouragement and financial support during the course of my field work. The valuable editorial criticism of E.D. Ward-Harris, Dr J.R. Maze (Department of Botany, University of British Columbia) and Harold Hosford (British Columbia Provincial Museum) is gratefully acknowledged. To Dr A.F. Szczawinski, Curator of Botany in the Provincial Museum, and R. Yorke Edwards, Director of the Museum, I owe a debt of gratitude for their support, advice and editorial counsel. The final manuscript was typed by Rosemary Patterson. Her assistance is sincerely appreciated.

The majority of the photographs were taken by my husband, Robert D. Turner, who also gave me unlimited moral support, not only during the writing of this book but through the months of field work preceding it.

N.J.T.
1975

PREFACE TO THE SECOND EDITION

Since this book was first published in 1975, not surprisingly, much has changed: many of the elders who contributed their knowledge to the book have passed away; logging and other impacts on the environment have accelerated; and yet, perhaps ironically, more has been learned about the intricate ecological web that binds us all together. Concern for the health of the environment and its resources is probably greater than it has ever been in British Columbia. As a result, more and more people are interested in the traditional knowledge of indigenous peoples, including the use of wild plant foods. Increasingly, efforts are being made to incorporate traditional philosophies and strategies for resource use into modern living.

Traditional foods have retained their significance, and in fact, are being recognized more and more for their importance to the well-being of aboriginal peoples. Aboriginal leaders, elders and educators have demonstrated their determination to retain this traditional knowledge, and to keep it as part of a living culture. Berry-picking, seaweed-gathering and other harvesting activities are enjoyed by aboriginal people of the 1990s, as much as in the 1970s. The nutritional and health values of traditional foods have been emphasized in the past two decades. This is demonstrated in projects such as the Nuxalk Food and Nutrition Program, which was carried out in the early 1980s by nutritionist Dr Harriet Kuhnlein in collaboration with the Nuxalk Nation and professional colleagues. Two of the elders who guided this program were Dr Margaret Siwallace (who received an honorary doctorate from the University of British Columbia in 1985) and Felicity Walkus – both were important contributors to this book. Many other elders and cultural experts have contributed their knowledge in research published since 1975. These people are named and acknowledged in more recent publications, such as *Traditional Plant*

Foods of Canadian Indigenous Peoples: Nutrition, Botany and Use (Kuhnlein and Turner 1991), which contains descriptions and nutrient values of traditional plant foods from across Canada.

In other sectors of society, interest in wild foods is increasing and taking new directions. Not only are people still enthusiastic about wild foods and how to harvest and use them, they are also interested in growing wild plants. Ecologically appropriate landscaping and gardening has become very popular. Not only do wild plants, once established, generally require less water and care than introduced species, they are good for teaching children about their natural environment, and they add both interest and practical value to the garden. The foremost reference for this endeavour is *Gardening with Native Plants of the Pacific Northwest* by Arthur Kruckeberg (1982). More is being written all the time on the propagation and cultivation of native plants. The University of British Columbia Botanical Garden in Vancouver has been a leader in developing new horticultural varieties of native species, including Kinnikinnick, Wild Strawberry, Evergreen Huckleberry and Red-flowering Currant. Some wild plants are already being grown for small-scale commercial use, in restaurants such as Sooke Harbour House near Victoria, where wild onions, Salal, Blue Camas and other edible wild plants are grown and used in specialty dishes served at this world-class country inn.

Another new area of interest surrounding edible wild plants is the use of wild edibles as non-timber forest products. Within the limits of sustainable harvesting and in ways that are culturally appropriate, wild foods and other plant materials can be applied by aboriginal peoples and others to the development of small-scale industries that do not remove large numbers of standing trees. These products, if carefully harvested, can allow forests to remain intact while still providing usable commodities. Non-timber forest products are being widely investigated by the United States Forest Service in the Pacific Northwest region. Wild mushroom harvests and decorative greens from forests have become major market goods in British Columbia. Other products, such as wild berries, may also have commercial potential. Specialty shops and restaurants may serve as outlets for wild berries, greens and teas. It will be necessary to monitor such uses very carefully, however, in order to ensure that they are not over-exploited, and that intellectual property rights of First Nations people are respected.

The books mentioned in this Preface and other recent publications and reports on plants in traditional diets in British Columbia are listed in a supplementary bibliography: Additional References. Only a few changes have been made to the text of this book. Throughout, however, we have used more up-to-date names for the aboriginal groups, and have substituted "aboriginal", "indigenous", "First Peoples" or "First Nations" for "Indian" and "native" in the original version. In addition, a new plant species, Pacific Hemlock-parsley (*Conioselinum pacificum*) is described, having been identified as the Indian Carrot of mid and north coastal peoples by Dr Brian Compton working with contemporary North Wakashan people and with historical records. Pacific Hemlock-parsley replaces Spring Gold (*Lomatium utriculatum*), whose use as a root vegetable remains problematic.

As well as all those acknowledged in the first edition, I would like to thank Gerry Truscott, Chief of Publishing Services, and Peter Macnair, Curator of Ethnology, at the Royal British Columbia Museum, and the people at the University of British Columbia Press for their work in the production of this second edition. I also acknowledge my husband, Bob Turner, for taking the berries photograph appearing on the cover, as well as many of the other photos in the book. Thanks to all the photographers whose images appear in this edition (see the copyright page for credits) and to Adolf Ceska, Curator of Botany at the Royal B.C. Museum for helping to gather them.

I am especially indebted to all those who patiently taught me about traditional plant foods. I would like to dedicate this edition to them, and to all those younger aboriginal people who have learned well from their parents and grandparents, continue to use traditional plant foods, and are teaching their own children about the richness of their heritage and environment.

Nancy J. Turner, Ph.D., FLS
Environmental Studies Program
University of Victoria
August 1995

Nuu-chah-nulth (Hesquiaht) woman picking Evergreen Huckleberries.
(RBCM PN4854.)

INTRODUCTION

In this age of pre-cooked instant foods with their innumerable vita-min/mineral supplements and chemical additives, many of us regard the eating practices of the original inhabitants of our country with admiration verging on envy. We conjure visions of rivers teaming with fish, and hillsides covered with luscious edible greenery and sweet, juicy berries – everything there for the taking. Realistically, these conditions, if they ever did exist, were only seasonal and local; harvesting wild foods and preparing them for winter storage were dif-ficult and time-consuming tasks. That First Peoples were able to sub-sist or, in many cases, thrive on a diet of wild plants and animals is a tribute to their ingenuity and industry.

In British Columbia, animal life – birds, mammals, fish and shell-fish – formed the bulk of First Peoples' diet, but plants provided an important nutritional supplement to their zoological fare. This book deals with the botanical component of the diet of coastal First Peoples. It contains, as far as possible, a systematic coverage of plants used as foods, flavourings and beverages, or for chewing or smoking. It includes botanical descriptions of the plants, notations on their habitat and distribution in coastal regions of the province, and details of their collection, preparation and use by the various indigenous groups on the coast. A second volume covers food plants of the province's interior and their use by interior First Peoples.

This handbook – and its companion, *Food Plants of Interior First Peoples* – have two purposes: first, to inform interested naturalists and outdoors enthusiasts of the wealth and diversity of wild edible plants to be found in the province, and second, for those interested in First Peoples' history and culture, to provide a record of species used by the various groups and of the different harvesting and preparation procedures. This book is designed primarily for use by non-profes-sionals. Where possible, technical terminology is avoided, and the botanical descriptions are illustrated with photographs for easier identification.

Many of the plants discussed in this book are abundant, quickly recognized and easily harvested, lending themselves to experimentation and use by enterprising individuals. Others are not recommended for use, but are included only in the interests of completeness and historical accuracy. In some cases, such as with plants having edible bulbs, harvesting for food necessitates destroying an entire plant to obtain a minimum of sustenance. Some of our most beautiful wild flowers – Calypso, Tiger Lily, Chocolate Lily and Yellow Dog-tooth Violet – can be inadvertently decimated within a small area by one or two natural-food enthusiasts. Similarly, the cambium and secondary phloem tissue of certain trees such as hemlock, spruce and cottonwood, is a valuable food source in an emergency, but its collection involves removing sections of bark, which injures the tree. Even the slightest exposure of the wood can render the tree susceptible to fungal rot or insect infestation; removing the bark around its entire circumference will kill a tree. Berries and nuts, on the other hand, can be gathered in quantity without injuring the plants or threatening the survival of the species.

Another danger in eating wild plants, far more serious to the consumer, is the possibility of poisoning through misuse or mistaken identification. Extreme caution must be taken in selecting and preparing plants for eating. The obvious risk is confusing an edible species with a similar-looking poisonous one. You can also poison yourself by eating a plant at the wrong stage of maturity or by eating the wrong part of a plant. Consuming a large quantity compounds the danger. Very few wild plants in British Columbia are fatal when eaten in small doses (some examples of deadly plants are Death Camas, Water Hemlock, and Indian Hellebore), but many plants, including some discussed as being edible in this book, can make you very ill if you eat a large amount or do not process them properly. Coastal First Peoples acquired their knowledge of plant foods through centuries of experimentation, driven by nutritional necessity and a quest for variety. Just as we have learned, through unfortunate experience, that a cupful of apple seeds contain enough cyanide to kill a person, that green-skinned potatoes can be highly toxic and that rhubarb leaves are extremely poisonous, despite the edibility of the stems, so First Peoples must have discovered that cooked lupine roots are good to eat but raw ones cause drunkenness, that Sea Milkwort roots cause nausea, and that the fertile shoots of horsetail are edible but the mature green vegetative shoots are not. Such details and special notes concerning the poisonous properties of certain plants should be carefully considered by those wishing to sample aboriginal plant foods.

Format

The plants in this volume are arranged in an order that is partially botanical and partially practical. They are organized first by major plant groups: algae, ferns and their relatives, gymnosperms (conifers and their relatives) and flowering plants. (Fungi, lichens, and mosses and their allies were not generally used as food by coastal First Peoples, so are not included.) Flowering plants are further divided into two subgroups: monocotyledons and dicotyledons. Within these major divisions, except in algae, the plants are classed in families, which are presented in alphabetical order. Plants in a given family are listed alphabetically by scientific name, which appears on the right-hand side of the page. The most common English name of the species appears on the left-hand side. The family name is shown below in parentheses.

Two appendixes are included. The first describes introduced and imported plant species that have been important food sources of coastal First Peoples in the period following contact with Europeans. Of course, aboriginal people today use as many types of fruits, vegetables and plant products as non-aboriginal people, but certain plants, such as turnips, potatoes and apples, were widely used even in the early days of European contact, and in some cases were major trading items. Almost all the plants in this appendix were given native names by at least one indigenous group on the coast, indicating a long-standing relationship between First Peoples and these imported species. The second appendix lists plants not mentioned in the main text that were considered to be poisonous by one or more coastal indigenous group. The major diagnostic features of these plants are given, along with details of coastal First Peoples' beliefs about them.

Sources of Information

Numerous reference sources were consulted in the preparation of this book. The botanical descriptions and notes on habitats and distribution were derived partially from personal observation, but were mainly compiled from several comprehensive regional floras. These include the five-volume work edited by C.L. Hitchcock, *Vascular Plants of the Pacific Northwest* (1955-69); J.A. Calder and R.L. Taylor's *Flora of the Queen Charlotte Islands,* Part 1 (1968); *Flora of Southern British Columbia* (1915) by J.K. Henry, and its supplement (1947) by J.W. Eastham; and the British Columbia Provincial Museum's handbooks: *The Ferns and Fern-allies of British Columbia* (1963), *The Heather Family of British Columbia* (1962), *The Lily Family of British Columbia* (1966), *Guide to Common Seaweeds of British Columbia* (1971), *The Rose Family of British Columbia* (1973) and *Guide to the Trees and Shrubs of British Columbia* (1973).

I obtained information on the actual uses of the plants as food by coastal First Peoples largely through personal contact with elderly members of contemporary aboriginal communities – people who could remember the days when many types of wild plants were still used extensively. I also consulted many reference sources. Most notable among these were Franz Boas' *Ethnology of the Kwakiutl* (1921), Philip Drucker's *The Northern and Central Nootkan Tribes* (1951), G.M. Sproat's *Scenes and Studies of Savage Life* (1868), Wilson Duff's *The Upper Stalo Indians* (1952), Wayne Suttles' *Katzie Ethnographic Notes* (1955) and R. Bouchard's unpublished manuscript, *Mainland Comox Plant Names* (1973). I obtained information on food plants of the First Peoples of western Washington from Erna Gunther's *Ethnobotany of Western Washington* (1945). The Additional References section at the back of this book contains more recent references to traditional plant foods.

The Physical Environment

This handbook deals specifically with coastal First Peoples of British Columbia and the edible plants growing in their territories. The areas of study are Vancouver Island, the Gulf Islands, Haida Gwaii (the Queen Charlotte Islands) and the coastal mainland north of the United States border, west of the Cascade and Coast Mountain ranges and south of the Alaska Panhandle. Many of the plants described also occur in coastal Alaska and Washington; some of their uses by neighbouring groups in those areas is discussed.

Most of the terrain in this area is extremely rugged: spectacular mountains and steep-sided valleys are characteristic of the coast. Deep fiords and inlets penetrate up to 80 kilometres inland. These, and the innumerable streams and rivers flowing down to the ocean, often provided the only feasible access to interior areas for indigenous peoples of the coast. Some lowlands (coastal plains and alluvial flood plains) also occur, as well as areas of gently sloping hills and plateaus. These areas contain lakes, swamps and peat bogs, which were frequented by the aboriginal people to collect certain types of plant foods not available on the immediate coast. Salt marshes, lagoons and estuarine flats were also important sources of edible plants.

Coastal First Peoples generally built their villages along the shoreline, often at river estuaries. Since their main transportation vehicle was the canoe, the ocean formed no barrier to them. In fact, it was like a highway, while the rugged slopes and dense forests of the land often posed more difficult obstacles. The numerous islands scattered along the coast were regularly visited and were often the sites of permanent villages.

The climate of coastal British Columbia is typically marine, with mild summer and winter temperatures. In the lowland areas, no month of the year has an average temperature below freezing. Vast quantities of water evaporate from the Pacific Ocean; they are carried shoreward by the prevailing westerlies and deposited on the mountain slopes in the form of heavy rain or snow. In many regions of the coast, precipitation averages over 250 centimetres annually. The mild climate of the coast, combined with the heavy precipitation, sustains a dense, luxurious growth of coniferous trees and associated plant species, which is appropriately called a coastal temperate rain forest.

Biologists recognize three major vegetation zones, technically known as biogeoclimatic zones, in the territory frequented by First Peoples of coastal British Columbia. The first, known as the Coastal Douglas-fir Zone, occurs on the leeward side of Vancouver Island, the Gulf Islands and the lowland areas of the adjacent mainland. The second, the Coastal Western Hemlock Zone, is found along the windward side of Vancouver Island, on the Queen Charlotte Islands, on the Mainland of the Strait of Georgia above 90 metres elevation (above the Coastal Douglas-fir Zone) and northward along the entire mainland coast below a range of about 1,000 metres in the south to 300 metres in the north. The third zone, the Mountain Hemlock Zone, occurs above the Coastal Western Hemlock Zone at sub-alpine elevations (between 900 and 1,700 metres in the south and between about 300 and 600 metres on the Alaskan Panhandle). A fourth zone in this region, the Alpine Tundra Zone, is above the tree-line, but it offers few traditional plant foods.

These three major zones differ climatically, as well as vegetationally. The Coastal Douglas-fir Zone, being in a rain-shadow area, is relatively dry, particularly during the summer months. Precipitation, mostly in the form of rain, averages 65 to 150 centimetres per year. In contrast, the Coastal Western Hemlock Zone has an average annual precipitation of 165 to 665 centimetres. The Mountain Hemlock Zone also has a high precipitation, averaging 180 to 430 centimetres annually, but much of it is in the form of snow. In the higher elevations of this zone, the snow cover often lasts until mid summer.

Certain combinations of plants characterize these vegetation zones, but many species grow in more than one of them. Some of the common trees of the Coastal Douglas-fir Zone, besides Douglas-fir (*Pseudotsuga menziesii*) itself, are Pacific Madrone (*Arbutus menziesii*), Garry Oak (*Quercus garryana*), Lodgepole Pine (*Pinus contorta*), Grand Fir (*Abies grandis*), Broad-leaved Maple *(Acer macrophyllum)* and Red Alder (*Alnus rubra*). Trees associated with Western Hemlock (*Tsuga heterophylla*) in the Coastal Western Hemlock Zone are Western Redcedar (*Thuja plicata*), Sitka Spruce (*Picea sitchensis*) and Silver Fir (*Abies amabilis*), as well as Red Alder. In the third zone, growing with Mountain Hemlock (*Tsuga mertensiana*), are trees such as Yellow-cedar (*Chamaecyparis nootkatensis*), Silver Fir and occasionally Subalpine Fir *(Abies lasiocarpa)*. You can learn more about these zones and their associated vegetation from *Ecosystems of British Columbia* (1991), edited by Del Meidinger and Jim Pojar, and *Plants of Coastal British Columbia* (1994), edited by Jim Pojar and Andy MacKinnon.

Many edible plant species, like the trees mentioned above, are more abundant in one zone than another, and so were more readily available to the people living in that zone than to those in another. A good example is Blue Camas, which is generally restricted on the British Columbia coast to the drier climate of the Coastal Douglas-fir Zone. Only the indigenous groups living in this zone (the people of southeastern Vancouver Island and the Gulf Islands) were able to use them to any extent, although other groups sometimes traded for them. Similarly, acorns (from Garry Oak), Chocolate Lily bulbs, Sticky Gooseberries, Red-flowering Currants and Blue Elderberries were available only to the people of the Coastal Douglas-fir Zone, while High-bush Cranberries, Indian Rice (Rice Root), Bunchberries, and Oval-leaved and Alaska blueberries were obtained primarily by the groups of the Coastal Western Hemlock Zone. Plants restricted to the Mountain Hemlock Zone were less available to almost all coastal First Peoples because of the difficulty getting to subalpine regions.

First Peoples of the Coast

The indigenous groups of the British Columbia coast, as discussed in this book, are as follows: Haida (Massett and Skidegate dialects), Haisla (includes Kitamaat, Kemano and Hanaksiala), Heiltsuk (previously called Northern Kwakuitl or Bella Bella), Tsimshian (includes Kitasoo, or Southern Tsimshian), Oweekeno, Kwakwaka'wakw (also called Kwagiulth; previously called Southern Kwakuitl), Nuu-chah-nulth (previously called Nootka; includes Ditidaht, previously called Nitinaht), Nuxalk (previously called Bella Coola), Comox (includes Sliammon), Sechelt, Squamish, Halq'emeylem (also called Halkomelem; includes Nanaimo, Chemainus, Cowichan, Musqueam and Sto:lo dialects) and Straits Salish (Saanich, Songhees, Clallam, T'souke and Semiahmoo dialects). The Tlingit of Alaska and several Washington groups are also included.

The territories occupied by these groups are shown on the map on page 8. You can obtain further information on the languages and cultural characteristics of these groups from *Northwest Coast* (1990), edited by Wayne Suttles, and from other publications provided in the References and Additional References. All of these groups are considered to be members of the same general cultural unit, known as the Northwest Coast Culture Area, and like other groups in Alaska, Washington, Oregon and northern California belonging in this Culture Area, they formerly shared a number of distinctive cultural traits, including a fishing and water-oriented economy, with special dependence on Pacific salmon and extensive use of Western Red-cedar for constructing dugout canoes, plank houses and kerfed storage boxes, and for manufacturing bark-fibre clothing, ropes, blankets and mats. For the latter set of items, the bark fibre of Yellow-cedar was also employed.

You will notice in the discussions under individual plant species that the types of edible plants used and the methods of preparing them often differ with each group of people. Part of this difference is accounted for by the presence or absence of certain plant species in a given region, but variations in use can also be due to the different cultural traditions. Each of the groups listed has a distinct language, history and set of cultural attributes, so that even when the edible plant resources available to two groups might be identical, their use may not be. Nevertheless, there are some obvious similarities in the use of plant foods among certain groups. These can frequently be attributed to historical ties between populations, often resulting from territorial proximity.

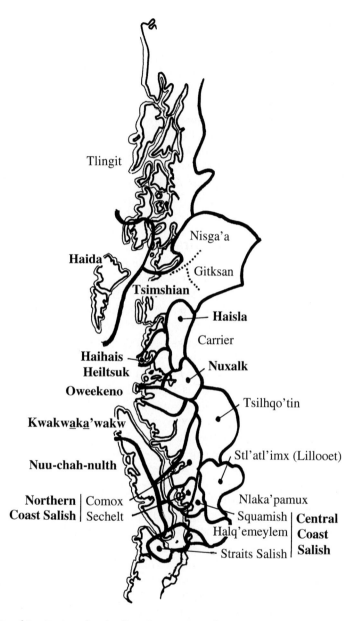

Traditional territories of major linguistic groups of coastal British Columbia. Major groups are in bold; subgroups and adjacent interior groups are also included.

Linguistic similarities per se do not seem particularly important in determining traditions involving edible plants. The last five groups named above, from Comox to Straits Salish, are all coastal members of the Salishan Language Family and show many similarities in the types of plants used as food and the methods of preparation employed. But these similarities are due less to the common origin of the languages than to the similar cultural traditions of these people, promoted by constant cultural and material interchange among them. The Nuxalk people are also a Salishan group, but are isolated from the other Salish populations, so their use of plant foods corresponds more closely to that of the neighbouring Heiltsuk, Haisla and Kwakwaka'wakw.

Plants in the Diet of First Peoples

No matter what specific types of plants were eaten by various indigenous groups and what methods were applied in gathering and preparing them, the basic kinds of plant foods involved are more or less standard. They include fruits (especially berries), green vegetables (sprouts, leaves and seaweeds), underground parts such as roots, bulbs, tubers and rhizomes, and cambium and inner bark tissues from certain trees. Of these, berries and seaweeds are still widely eaten by present First Nations populations; other types of foods are not as commonly used, and generally have been unable to compete with the convenience and flavour of domesticated greens, root vegetables and commercially available foods.

Plant products contributed only a part of the total food intake of coastal First Peoples; as mentioned earlier, animal products were far more important in terms of quantities consumed. There is no doubt, however, that the nutritional diversity provided by native plants was a significant factor in determining the number of people who could survive on the west coast. The aboriginal population of the coast before the coming of Europeans is now estimated to be over 100,000 – the densest aboriginal population of any region in Canada.

One component of the aboriginal diet, carbohydrates, was in short supply, especially in the middle and northern regions of the coast where Blue Camas does not grow. Although several varieties of roots, rhizomes and bulbs were available in these regions, the amounts consumed were apparently relatively small compared to the total food intake. In *The Northern and Central Nootkan Tribes* (1951), Philip

Drucker estimates that the average Nuu-chah-nulth family ate only 12 meals of roots in a year, but this estimation seems low based on the recollections of contemporary elders. Still, the Nuu-chah-nulth, Kwakwaka'wakw, Nuxalk, Haida and Coast Tsimshian must have generally fared poorly in carbohydrates. Evidently, they replaced carbohydrates largely with animal fats and oils, as did aboriginal peoples in the Arctic. The most notable carbohydrate substitute is "Grease", a clear oil rendered from a small fish, the Eulachon (or Oolichan). The Eulachon is sometimes called the candle fish, because it is so oily that one can string a wick through it and light it like a candle. Eulachon grease was – and still is – a major part of the diet of the middle and northern groups. It is used in the same manner as others use butter or margarine. It is clear and yellowish, with a taste, according to some, reminiscent of halibut-liver oil. Most people of European descent find it strong tasting, but aboriginal people of the west coast relish it. Traditionally, Eulachon grease is eaten with other foods: berries, raw or cooked, are dipped in it, as are green sprouts and cooked roots; sometimes it is mixed right into the food; and some types of fruits are stored in it.

As you might appreciate, when commercial carbohydrates (flour, rice, potatoes, turnips, carrots and beans) were introduced, they attained immediate popularity with coastal First Peoples.

Vegetable protein was even more limited than carbohydrates in the traditional diet, but the shortage was more than compensated for by the abundance of animal protein. Animal products, such as dried salmon, herring spawn, clams and deer meat, were eaten with almost every vegetable dish. Seaweeds and greens, such as Cow Parsnip, Fireweed and Salmonberry sprouts, and the nutrient-rich cambium and inner bark tissues of hemlock, cottonwood and other trees provided necessary vitamins and minerals, just as green vegetables do in our modern diet.

In comparison to the seemingly limitless varieties of candies and desserts we consume today, the confections available to the coastal First Peoples were meagre indeed. Berries were their main source of sugar, and many of these are tart and had to be mixed with more palatable types. A widely relished dessert, known today as "Indian ice-cream", was made by whipping Soapberries mixed with water into a stiff froth. The berries themselves are so bitter few people can eat more than one. The flavour of the froth is somewhat diluted; it is still disagreeable to those unaccustomed to eating it, but once you acquire a taste for it, it is delicious. Indian ice-cream was usually sweetened by adding Saskatoon or Salal berries, and one or two groups sweetened it with Licorice Fern rhizomes.

It is not surprising that the introduction of sugar and molasses by the first European traders resulted in an almost revolutionary change in the eating habits of coastal First Peoples. Sugar became a treasured product, an all-purpose condiment rivalled in popularity only by the ever-present Grease. It was mixed in Indian ice-cream (although too much is said to ruin the flavour), and like Grease, it was added to berries, green vegetables, roots, rhizomes and bulbs. Many aboriginal people even added large amounts to Labrador Tea, which is pleasant-tasting without sweetening. The coming of Europeans was detrimental to the lives of the First Peoples in many ways, but one pleasure, at least, was the gift of sugar.

Harvesting Food Plants

Among coastal First Peoples, as in many societies, the gathering of vegetable foods was mainly the responsibility of the women, while the men occupied themselves with hunting and fishing. Women did most of the cooking and preparing the food for winter storage, though men would often help. Before the harvest season began, the women of a village had to make sure their equipment was in good order. They repaired their berry baskets or made new ones if the old baskets were too fragile to last over the winter.

When berries were ripe for picking or roots were ready to be dug, a woman had to work ceaselessly during the daylight hours to finish before the next lot was due to harvest. Her day started before sunrise. Before setting out to harvest, she assembled all her equipment: kneeling mats, "back-protecting" mats to wear while digging roots, hats for protection against the sun, tump-lines to help carry the heavy baskets and boxes, digging-sticks, combs for huckleberries, hooks for elderberries and any other specialized implements.

Each woman had her own favourite berry patches and root-digging grounds where she would go year after year. Sometimes these grounds were actually "owned" by her or members of her family, and others had to ask permission or pay a fee to use them, but ordinarily they were used on a first-come-first-served basis. Often, the women had to travel long distances by foot or canoe to reach their harvesting grounds and then carry their produce back to the village or summer camp. On major expeditions, women would travel in groups or with their immediate families; shorter journeys were made alone.

Hesquiaht berry picker boarding her canoe. (RBCM PN5417.)

After a light breakfast, perhaps of dried salmon and a few leftover roots, the berry-picker or root-digger would carry her baskets and other equipment down the beach to her canoe just as dawn began to break. A nursing mother would take her baby with her; if she had older children, she would leave them with a grandmother or aunt. The harvester might paddle her canoe to an island, up the estuary of a river or around a rocky point to some quiet cove or lagoon, depending on the type of food she sought. When she reached her destination, she would beach her canoe and carry her containers and implements to the harvesting grounds. She might stop along the way and chew up some Mountain Goat tallow, spreading it thickly over her hands and face to protect herself against the inevitable swarms of mosquitoes and biting flies, which at times must have made her work unbearable.

She carried several sizes of baskets for berry-picking. Kwakwaka'wakw women used three types – a large "swallowing" basket, a "middle one" and a small or "front" basket that was slung round the neck, leaving her hands free. She picked berries into this small basket, and when it was full, emptied it into the swallowing basket and the middle one until they were both full. By this time the day was nearly over. After filling the front basket for the last time, she made covers for her baskets with branches or Skunk Cabbage leaves, then carried her produce back to her canoe. During the day, if she was hungry, she might nibble one or two berries; but she knew that the berry spirits frowned upon women who ate while they picked, and on another day her luck might be bad if she were too greedy and did not respect the fruit she harvested. When she returned home, she would summon her husband to help her carry the baskets up to the house, and finally would allow herself the luxury of food and rest.

Digging roots and bulbs was even more laborious than gathering berries. The digger had to crouch or kneel on a thin mat for hours at

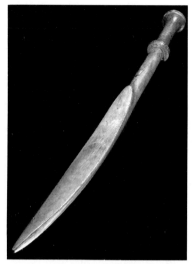

Hesquiaht woman digging roots. (BCARS D-08314.)

Kwakwaka'wakw digging stick made of yew wood. (RBCM CPN496).

a time, thrusting her digging-stick into the ground, prying up earth and roots, carefully extricating the roots without breaking them, digging, prying, extracting, until her muscles were so stiff and her hands so sore she could hardly move them. It took four or five days of this kind of toil to harvest a crop of Clover or Cinquefoil roots to last a family over the winter and still have enough to contribute to a communal feast during the winter dance season. Root crops were carefully managed. Diggers selected only the larger roots, and replanted the smaller ones and fragments so they would continue growing. Some people maintained their root-digging grounds like gardens. They might, for example, periodically burn over their camas beds to enhance their productivity.

Preparation of Plant Foods

Harvesting plant foods was only the beginning of a woman's work. Some foods (green sprouts and certain types of berries, such as Salmonberries) were eaten fresh, soon after they were gathered; but most plant foods had to be prepared for storage, to be used later in the winter when no fresh produce was available. To prepare berries, she sorted, de-stemmed and mashed them, then cooked them with red-hot stones. She poured the hot mash into rectangular wooden frames (about 60 x 30 x 2 cm) set on broad Skunk Cabbage leaves and place them side by side on a long rack, usually near a fire, so that the berries dried slowly. After several days, the berries in the moulds solidified into cakes that could be folded or rolled. They were stored in boxes in a cool part of the house until they were needed.

To use the berries in winter, the woman soaked them in water overnight, mashed them, and often mixed them with other berries and (at least in the middle and northern regions) Eulachon Grease. These reconstituted berries were said to taste just like fresh-picked fruit.

Tree cambium and secondary phloem was also dried in cakes, except that of cottonwood, which soured after a few days. Strips of cambium were prepared for storage by cooking them in steaming pits, then pounding them with rock hammers to soften them before drying. Dried cambium also had to be soaked before it could be eaten, and it was often mixed with Grease. Edible seaweeds were dried in sheets on the rocks or packed in layers in wooden boxes.

Bulbs, roots and rhizomes had to be cleaned, sorted and dried to the point where they would not rot or become mouldy. In dry weather, the harvesters spread them out on mats, often right at the site where they dug them up, then placed them in fibre bags or cedar boxes. Most underground parts required prolonged boiling or steam-cooking before they could be eaten. Before metal pots and kettles were available, coastal aboriginal people often boiled water in bent-wood boxes. They made these tall wooden boxes by an ingenious process of steaming or soaking and bending a cedar board into a four-sided structure with only one joint; they fitted the bent board with a bottom and cover, sewing the open seams with spruce-root twine. A bent-wood box was watertight, and could be used equally well for storing dried products, fruits in water and Grease. It could also be used for cooking. The cook simply added red-hot stones to the water and food in the box until the mixture began to boil, then put the cover on and left it until the food was cooked.

Coastal First Peoples also cooked with steam in "earth-ovens". First they dug a large hole in the earth or sand and lined it with stones. Then they kindled a fire in the pit and kept it burning until the stones were red hot. After removing the ashes and unburned wood, they placed a layer of damp vegetation (seaweed or leaves, fern fronds, and Salal or alder branches) over the rocks, then spread the bulbs, roots or whatever food they wanted to cook over this layer. They added another layer of damp vegetation, another of food, and so on until the pit was full. Finally, they covered it with old mats and piled earth over the top. They might add extra water, then leave the food to cook in the oven. The hot rocks caused the damp vegetation to steam, and the earth and mats held the heat in; the food cooked slowly but steadily. The cooks might add more water through a hole in the top if the vegetation dried out. After one or two nights, depending on the type of food cooking, the meal was ready, or the food could be dried for storage.

Kwakwa̲ka'wakw cedar bent-wood storage box. (RBCM CPN 12866).

Large portions of the produce a woman laboured so hard to gather and store were contributed to the general coffers of the village for distribution at communal feasts and potlatches. Ironically, women were sometimes excluded from such feasts, especially in Kwakwa̲ka'-wakw society. If a woman was lucky, her husband might bring home some of the leftovers for her; but this did not always happen, for at some feasts, etiquette required that the guest finish all the food placed in front of him. His wife, however, had the satisfaction of knowing that her toils increased the prestige of the chief and, indirectly, of herself and other members of the village.

Food Plants Throughout the Seasons

The seasonal movements of coastal First Peoples were largely dependent on the types of food available at a particular time and the localities where they could be obtained. During the winter months the tribes remained in their permanent villages, living off stored food and partaking of the various social activities for which northwest coast First Peoples are famous – potlatches, spirit dancing, games and feasts. Towards the end of the winter, supplies became short and famine was not uncommon, especially if the previous year had been a bad one for salmon, game or berries. Late winter was the most difficult time of the year; people had to resort to emergency foods not normally eaten, such as fern root stocks. At the first sign of spring, the villages broke up into small family units to begin the never-ending search for wholesome food and materials for manufacture.

Throughout the growing season until well into the fall, families would travel from place to place within the territory of the village group, stopping at one spot for two weeks, and another for a month or more, occasionally travelling to distant villages to trade for foodstuffs not found in their own area.

The first plant foods available in spring were roots, such as lupines, Sea Milkwort, "Wild Carrot" and Springbank Clover, although these could also be harvested in fall. The Kwakwa̲ka̲'wakw of Alert Bay and Fort Rupert on Vancouver Island used to journey each spring to Knight and Kingcome Inlets on the mainland to obtain these roots, and also to acquire their year's supply of Grease, since the Eulachon run occurs there in late March. Various green vegetables (Salmonberry and Thimbleberry sprouts, nettles, Fireweed shoots and Cow Parsnip stalks) were at their prime in spring. Coastal First Peoples gathered and ate them fresh as a welcome change from the meagre diet of late winter. They also collected Red Laver seaweed from the rocks along the shore. Later in spring, they scraped cambium off the bark and wood of hemlock, cottonwood and other trees to eat fresh or cook and store for future use.

In early summer the berries and fruits started to ripen, beginning with Salmonberries and wild strawberries, followed by huckleberries, blueberries, blackberries, Saskatoon Berries, Soapberries, gooseberries, currants, elderberries, wild raspberries, Blackcaps, Thimbleberries, and most notably, Salal berries. Coastal First Peoples often held ceremonies to celebrate the ripening of each kind of fruit. Even today, the ripening of berries is an exciting time and many aboriginal families still go out to pick them, just as their ancestors did.

Towards the end of the summer, most types of bulbs, including Blue Camas, wild onions and Indian Rice (*Fritillaria* spp.) were ready to be harvested, although the digging season varied considerably from group to group. In the autumn months, aboriginal harvesters occupied themselves with digging up more Springbank Clover rhizomes, Pacific Cinquefoil roots, fern rhizomes, lupine roots and other types of underground parts, and with gathering the late-ripening fruits – Hazelnuts, crabapples, cranberries, Kinnikinnick berries, rose hips and Evergreen Huckleberries. They did not usually dry these fruits in cakes as they did the summer berries, but ate them fresh or cooked, or stored them in water or oil in wooden storage boxes. The practice of storing fruits in water was especially common among the middle and northern indigenous groups (see the discussion under Wild Crabapple).

Finally, after months of transience, the families converged again on their winter villages, bringing with them the products of their industry to share and enjoy during the winter months.

Food Plants and Etiquette

Tradition is an important component of the coastal First Peoples' lifestyle. The use of plant foods, like other aspects of culture, was subject to numerous customs and regulations, particularly in societies that had a highly formalized social structure, with elaborate ceremonies and strict adherence to rules of etiquette and protocol. The Kwakwaka'wakw people observed many controls on their lives, especially during the winter dance season; many of these concerned plant foods. Only certain foods and combinations of foods could be served at feasts. Each type of root or berry had to be eaten in a certain way. At Salal berry feasts, the guests were called four times, while at Indian Plum feasts they were called only twice. The guests sang special feast songs when they were eating Rice Root, but did not sing when they ate Bunchberries. They drank water after an elderberry feast, but never after a gooseberry feast. Leftover Pacific Cinquefoil roots could be taken home to the wives, but Clover roots had to be completely finished at the feast. Salmonberry shoots were eaten with sticky salmon spawn, while Clover roots were eaten with scorched dried salmon. Only chiefs were allowed to eat pure Salal berry cakes and long Cinquefoil roots; the commoners ate Salal cakes mashed with elderberries and short Cinquefoil roots. Tradition also dictated whether spoons were used, how many people ate from each dish, whether shredded cedar bark was provided for wiping the hands, and who could attend each feast. In his *Ethnology of the Kwakiutl* (1921), Franz Boas recorded these and other traditions concerning the use of plant foods in great detail.

Trading Food Plants

Even in the days before Europeans arrived, the trading of resources was widely practised by coastal First Peoples, especially between local villages. Also, the major river valleys provided commercial links between coastal and interior peoples. Trading increased in both frequency and quantity after the arrival of Europeans, who introduced new technology and new items for exchange. Plant products, especially plant foods, were important trading items before and after European contact.

On the southern coast, the Straits Salish traded camas bulbs to the Nuu-chah-nulth, Kwakwaka'wakw and Sto:lo of the Fraser Valley. The Sto:lo in turn traded Bog Cranberries, blueberries and Wapato tubers to the Squamish and Straits Salish. They also traded with the Nlaka'pamux (previously called Thompson Salish) in the interior, obtaining from them a special sweet variety of Saskatoon Berry as well as Soapberries and interior root vegetables. The Kwakwaka'-wakw traded dried seaweed, High-bush Cranberries and crabapples to the Comox, Sechelt and Nuxalk, who in turn traded these and other products to the Ulkatcho Carrier and Tsilhqot'in (Chilcotin) people of the interior. The Sechelt traded for Soapberries with the Lillooet of the Pemberton Valley. The Haida traded dried seaweed, crabapples and native tobacco (*Nicotiana* sp.) to the Tsimshian in return for Soapberries, Cloudberries, Grease and smoked Eulachons. The Massett Haida acquired Soapberries from the Tlingit in Alaska. Within the last two centuries, potatoes, rice, turnips, apples and many other imported fruits and vegetables became valuable as articles of trade.

Seaweed gatherer (BCARS D-08316).

SEAWEEDS
(Marine Algae)

Giant Kelp	*Macrocystis integrifolia* **Bory**
(Brown Algae)	**(Phaeophyta)**

Botanical Description

One of the largest marine algae, Giant Kelp is deep greenish brown with several stipes (stems) attached to a single holdfast. Large, flat leaf-like blades, generally 35 to 40 cm long and 5 to 10 cm wide, depending on maturity, arise at intervals along the stipe. The blades have an irregular or

wavy surface and a toothed edge, and taper abruptly at the base. Each is held at the surface of the water by a small, spherical float at its base.

Habitat: rocks in the upper subtidal zone, to a depth of about 7 metres, usually in large beds in areas close to the open ocean, but not directly exposed to heavy surf.

Distribution in British Columbia: along the Coast, from Vancouver Island to Alaska, but not in sheltered inlets like the one at the mouth of the Bella Coola River.

Aboriginal Use

In some localities, during their spawning season from March to June, Pacific Herring deposit thick layers (up to 2 cm) of spawn on both surfaces of Giant Kelp blades. Middle and northern coastal First

Dried Giant Kelp with herring spawn.

Peoples (but apparently not Coast Salish groups) harvest the spawn-covered blades. The Kwakwaka'wakw sometimes pick the blades beforehand, weight them with rocks, and place them under the water near river mouths to increase the likelihood of herring spawning on them. After the herring start to spawn, the eggs are allowed to accumulate for about two days before the blades are ready to harvest. Other groups collect herring spawn from Eelgrass leaves, submerged branches of Western Hemlock or Sitka Spruce and some other types of seaweed such as Boa Kelp (*Egregia menziesii*).

Coastal First Peoples gathered spawn-covered Giant Kelp from canoes. They laid the kelp blades on rocks to dry in the sun, then bundled them in packages of about ten blades each and stored them for winter or sold them to neighbouring groups. To prepare kelp with herring spawn for eating, the cook soaked them overnight, broke them into bite-sized pieces and boiled the pieces in cedar boxes. At feasts, kelp with herring spawn was eaten with Grease, usually with a special spoon.

The Haida at Skidegate, the Heiltsuk and some other peoples still eat herring spawn on kelp, although the Federal Fisheries Department has discouraged this practice. Non-aboriginal people are not allowed to eat it at all. Nowadays, aboriginal people preserve the spawn-laden blades by packing them in salt or freezing them. Sometimes they cut the blades into thin strips, dry them to the consistency of rubber bands and eat them as snacks − these are special treats for children, who carry them to school in their pockets to eat at recess. But the usual method of preparing them is to fry them in bacon grease or butter until they are crisp and lightly browned on both sides. They are eaten with a knife and fork, like pancakes. They have a rich salty flavour and an unusual crunchy texture − soft and slightly rubbery.

In the 1990s, herring are not as plentiful as they used to be; many people blame the commercial herring-roe fishery, in which huge quantities of Pacific Herring are caught and the roe removed, mostly for shipment to Japan. In 1995, some aboriginal peoples were unable to harvest any quantity of herring roe on kelp.

Red Laver
(Red Algae)

Porphyra abbottae Krishnamurthy
(Rhodophyta)

Other Name: Edible Seaweed.

Botanical Description

Red Laver has a thin membranous blade, broad and irregularly shaped. When fresh, it is reddish-purple or greenish, having the consistency of cellophane. When dry, it is black and brittle. The blades are only one or two cell-layers thick. The young plants, when ready for harvesting, are about 10 cm long, but mature specimens can attain a height of 150 cm. *Porphyra abbottae* was formerly called *P. perforata.*

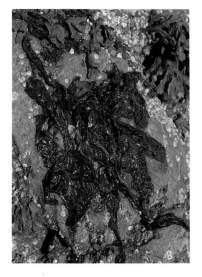

Habitat: rocks in the lower intertidal zone, in sheltered waters.

Distribution in British Columbia: along the entire coast, from Vancouver Island to Alaska.

Aboriginal Use

Many coastal groups, especially middle and northern groups, use Red Laver as food. They gather young plants from the rocks at low tide in spring, usually in May.

An old method of curing them, employed by the Kwakwa̱ka'wakw and Haida, was to partially dry them, allowing them to ferment slightly, and then press them into tall cedar boxes in layers interspersed with Western Red-cedar boughs to add flavouring. Sometimes they added an additional flavouring made from the juice of chewed rock chitons (marine shellfish). They left the packed boxes, weighted with rocks, for about a month, then unpacked them and repeated the entire process up to three times. The finished seaweed cakes, about 2 cm thick, were stored in boxes for winter. To prepare them, the cook tore the cakes into strips and chopped them into small pieces with an adze, then chewed the pieces, soaked them in water and boiled them. Red Laver was served in small dishes with Grease, boiled Dog (Chum) Salmon or boiled clams. According to Kwakwa̲ka̲'wakw etiquette, one could drink water after eating seaweed at a feast, but not before.

Another method used by the Kwakwa̲ka̲'wakw to prepare this seaweed was to hang individual blades on a drying-rack above a fire, allowing them to brown lightly, and then pound the dried blades into a fine powder. The powder could be mixed with water and boiled, or whipped into a froth and eaten as a dessert.

The simplest method of curing Red Laver, commonly used at present, is to spread it out on rocks in the sun. When dry, it is broken into small popcorn-size pieces (as shown in the photograph), which can be stored in buckets or cans. It can be eaten dried as a confection, or boiled with Grease, halibut heads, clams or creamed corn. It is a good laxative and health food.

Red Laver has been – and still is – a common trading item. Interior groups, such as the Carrier and Tsilhqot'in, used it as a medicine for goitre, an affliction caused by iodine deficiency. Central Coast Salish groups used to sell it to the Chinese and Japanese in the early part of the century. In 1975, a two-kilogram pail of dried seaweed cost about $5; in the 1990s it is substantially more expensive.

Red Laver "popcorn".

Coastal First Peoples ate several other kinds of seaweed, but Red Laver was the most common. Two related species, identified by alogologist Dr Sandra Lindstrom from samples of Haida "winter seaweed", are *P. torta* and *P. pseudolanceolata*.

FERNS AND THEIR RELATIVES
(Pteridophyta)

Giant Horsetail
Common Horsetail
(Horesetail Family)

Equisetum telmateia **Ehrh.**
E. arvense L.
(Equisetaceae)

Other Names: Mare's Tail, Scouring Rush.

Botanical Description
Giant and Common horsetails are perennial herbs with long, branching rhizomes. The stems are annual, jointed, hollow and rough to the touch; there are two types: light-coloured non-branching fertile shoots that appear in early spring and soon wither, and green sterile shoots with generally whorled branches that appear after the fertile shoots and remain until autumn. The leaves on both types of stems are reduced to scale-like appendages fused to form a sheath at each joint. Giant Horsetail is the larger of the two. The average length of its fertile and sterile stems are 20 cm and 45 cm respectively. Those of Common Horsetail

Giant Horsetail, showing vegetative shoots and dying fertile shoot.

average 15 cm and 25 cm. *Equisetum telmateia* is also known as *E. maximum.*

23

Habitat: low, wet ground, such as ditches and seepage areas; Common Horsetail is more tolerant of sunlight and poor soil conditions, and often grows in weedy habitats.

Distribution in British Columbia: Giant Horsetail is widely distributed along the coast, but does not occur east of the coastal mountains; Common Horsetail is common throughout the province.

Aboriginal Use
The succulent fertile shoots of both species were eaten fresh or boiled by several Coast Salish groups, including Sechelt, Squamish, Straits Salish and probably Halq'emeylem. The Nuu-chah-nulth and a number of groups in western Washington also ate them. The tough outer fibres were peeled off or chewed and discarded. The Saanich people thought the shoots were good for the blood. The Squamish used to drink the water from the hollow stem segments of Giant Horsetail. The Ditidaht and possibly other Nuu-chah-nulth groups also ate the vegetative shoots, cleaned of their sheathing, leaves and branches, but only when they were young and tightly compacted.

Warning
Common Horestail (*E. arvense*) is known to be toxic to livestock, causing weakness, trembling, and in extreme cases, coma and death. The exact poison is still unknown, but the symptoms are similar to Bracken Fern poisoning, where the enzyme thiaminase is involved. Never eat the green vegetative shoots, and eat the fertile shoots only in small quantities with extreme caution.

Lady Fern
(Fern Family)

Athyrium filix-femina (L.) Roth.
(Polypodiaceae)

Botanical Description

Lady Fern is a perennial with stout, erect rhizomes. The fronds are delicate, erect, clustered and deciduous, frequently a metre or more in height. The longest pinnae are those near the mid-section of the frond. Pinnae and pinnules are numerous. The stems are straw-coloured and scaly. The sori, when present, are numerous, small and usually horseshoe-shaped. Lady Fern is highly variable in size, shape and colour.

Habitat: damp, shady places, from shaded forest to open marsh; frequently found in association with Skunk Cabbage.

Distribution in British Columbia: in suitable habitats throughout the province.

Aboriginal Use

The Squamish and the Straits Salish in Washington steamed and ate the young shoots (fiddleheads). There are a number of reports of the rootstocks being steamed in pits and eaten. But it is likely that these references pertain to Spiny Wood Fern, widely considered the edible species, and not Lady Fern (see Turner et al, 1992, listed in Additional References).

Spiny Wood Fern
Dryopteris expansa
(K. Presl) Fraser-Jenkins & Jermy
and related species, including   *Dryopteris austriaca*
(Jacq.) Woynar ex Schinz & Thell.
(Fern Family)   (Polypodiaceae)

Botanical Description

Spiny Wood Fern is a perennial with stout, erect rhizomes. The fronds are delicate, erect, 30 to 50 cm in height, generally triangular, clustered and usually deciduous.

The lowermost pinnae are asymmetrical, but triangular. The pinnules are numerous and toothed. The stems are light-green with brown scales. The sori, when present, are on the undersurface of the frond and are small, round and indented.

Habitat: common in cool, moist woods, often on rotten logs and tree stumps.

Distribution in British Columbia: Spiny Wood Fern and its close relatives are among the most widespread ferns in the province, growing from sea-level to the tree-line, especially west of the Cascade Mountains.

Aboriginal Use

The Nuu-chah-nulth, Haida, Kwakwaka'wakw and a number of Washington groups, such as the Cowlitz, dug up rhizomes in the fall and ate them steamed. Other coastal groups in British Columbia also used them, as did the Nlaka'pamux (Thompson), Carrier, Gitskan and Nisga'a. In earlier times, the Haida steamed them in pits overnight and ate them with Grease; more recently, they boiled them in kettles for many hours. Raw rhizomes are bitter, but when cooked, they are said to be sweet-tasting. Details of the use of this important fern and of the difficulties identifying it are provided in a recent article by Turner et al (1993; cited in Additional References).

In the first edition of this book, Male Fern (*D. filix-mas*) was given as another edible fern species, eaten by the Nuxalk and others. But recently, Nuxalk elders have identified Spiny Wood Fern as the more commonly eaten type. They dug up the pineapple-like rhizomes of the Spiny Wood Fern around the end of September. At this time, the rhizomes are surrounded by scaly, finger-like projections, which are actually the beginning of next year's growth. If the projections are flat and dark inside, the rhizomes are not good to eat; but if they are round, fleshy and light-coloured, the rhizomes are edible. They were cooked overnight in steaming pits, or steamed in kettles. The Kwakwaka'wakw sometimes covered them with red ochre and roasted them on a hemlock stick over an open fire. The finger-like projections could be broken off, peeled like bananas and eaten with Grease or "stink egg" (fermented salmon roe). Some aboriginal people compare the taste of Spiny Wood Fern rhizomes to that of sweet potatoes.

The rhizomes of this species or Male Fern can also be eaten raw. The Nuxalk say they are good for losing weight and for curing sickness from eating poisonous plants or shellfish infected with red tide. But the rhizomes are bitter and have strong laxative properties. People of European background have used them as a vermifugant (de-worming medicine).

Licorice Fern
(Fern Family)

Polypodium glycyrrhiza D.C. Eat.
(Polypodiaceae)

Other Name: Polypody Fern.

Botanical Description

Licorice Fern is relatively small, usually 20 to 30 cm tall. It is so named for its licorice-flavoured rhizomes. The rhizomes are perennial, often more than 15 cm long, roundish, about 5 mm thick, branching and shallow; they are yellowish-green, scaly at the growing tips and bear wiry,  black rhizoids. The fronds are single, coarse and light green. They are often deciduous in the dry summer, producing fronds again in autumn. The pinnae are generally in 10 to 20 offset pairs, toothed, pointed and diminishing in length at the tip of the frond but otherwise about equal in length. The sori are round, orange, lacking indusia, occurring in two rows along the backs of the pinnae, especially the uppermost ones. *Polypodium glycyrrhiza* is also known as *P. vulgare* L. var. *occidentale.*

Habitat: on moist rocks and tree trunks, and in moss, from lowlands to subalpine areas; widespread within its range.

Distribution in British Columbia: restricted to the west side of the Cascade Mountains. Its close relative, *P. hesperium*, occurs on the coast and in the interior; it has smaller fronds and rounded pinnae.

Aboriginal Use

Licorice Fern rhizomes have a strong licorice taste and were used medicinally for colds and sore throats by many coastal groups. Most aboriginal people did not eat the rhizomes as food, but the Squamish, Sechelt, Comox, Nuxalk and Haida chewed them for the flavour. The first three groups used them as an appetiser, especially for children who would not eat. The Mainland Comox also used them to flavour Labrador Tea leaves. The Haida sometimes ate them before drinking water to make the water taste sweet. The Saanich may have used them as a sugar substitute to sweeten food and bitter-tasting medicine; they also ate them in small quantities, fresh or dried for winter.

Information in the first edition on Kwakwa̱ka'wakw use of Licorice Fern as winter food evidently refers to Spiny Wood Fern rhizomes. Boas (1921) identified the fern as *Polypodium*, but the Kwakwala name is for *Dryopteris.*

Licorice Fern rhizomes.

Sword Fern
(Fern Family)

Polystichum munitum (Kaulf.) K. Presl
(Polypodiaceae)

Botanical Description

The Sword Fern is a perennial with stout, fleshy, scaled rhizomes. The fronds are coarse, stiffly erect, dark green, clumped and evergreen. They vary in length, depending on habitat, but in forested areas average 60 cm. The stems are greenish and scaly. The pinnae are numerous, alternate, toothed and attached to the stem at a single point. Each has a prominent projection or "hilt" at the base on the upper edge. The sori are numerous, usually occurring in two rows on the undersurface of the upper pinnae, with indusia.

Habitat: common in damp, rich woods and shaded slopes, but also occurs on open rocky exposures; generally confined to lowland forests.

Distribution in British Columbia: widespread and extremely common west of the coastal mountains; a dominant fern in lowland coastal forests rich in humus.

Aboriginal Use

The Squamish, Sechelt, Nuu-chah-nulth, Kwakwa̲ka'wakw and Haida used the large Sword Fern rhizomes as food — but not the Comox, according to Bouchard (1973); in Washington, the Quileute, Makah and Clallam ate them. The rhizomes were usually dug up in the spring before the new leaves sprouted. They were cooked in open fires or steaming pits, then peeled and eaten, usually with Grease or dried salmon eggs. The Nuu-chah-nulth ate them especially to cure diarrhoea. Apparently, most of these groups regarded Sword Fern rhizomes as starvation food only, and preferred Spiny Wood Fern rhizomes when available. Young Sword Fern rhizomes, too small to eat, and the rhizomes of Deer Fern (*Blechnum spicant*) were called "scabby-girl" in Massett Haida because they were "no good".

Bracken Fern
(Fern Family)

Pteridium aquilinum (L.) Kuhn
(Polypodiaceae)

Botanical Description
Bracken Fern is the largest and most common fern in the province. It is often more than 150 cm tall. The rhizomes are perennial, often 20 cm deep, running horizontally for long distances, frequently branching. They are round in cross-section, about as thick as a man's middle finger, black outside, and white and glutinous inside with tough longitudinal fibres in the centre. The fronds are borne individually along the rhizome, having tall, smooth, light-green stems and coarsely branching pinnae. The fronds and lower pinnae are broadly triangular in shape. The pinnules are numerous and deeply toothed, and the sori, when present, are marginal and mostly continuous.

Habitat: a variety, but usually in open forests and clearings at lower elevations.

Distribution in British Columbia: generally throughout the province, except at high elevations.

Aboriginal Use
The Nuu-chah-nulth and Sechelt, and also some Washington groups, boiled and ate the fiddleheads of Bracken Fern. Virtually all coastal indigenous groups use the rhizomes as food. Most dug them up in late fall or winter, although the Nuxalk harvested them in summer. They coiled up the rhizomes and allowed them to dry. Later, they roasted them in an open fire until the outer skin could be peeled off, then pounded the inner parts with a stick. After removing the tough, central fibres, they ate the whitish starchy inside, usually with fish eggs or oil, because it was constipating. The Saanich ate it with seal oil, from a horse-clam shell, after a meat course.

The Kwakwaka'wakw broke the rhizomes into pieces four finger-widths long and ate them with salmon spawn or Grease. They believed that only old women should dig Bracken rhizomes, because it would make young women sick. The Nuu-chah-nulth roasted the roots only if there were too few to steam in an underground pit. They often chewed the cooked rhizomes with dried salmon eggs, without removing the outer skin or the inner fibres, spitting these out afterwards to be saved as tinder for lighting fires. The Haida also steamed them in pits, or recently, in large pots, when there were too many to roast. Barnett (1955) states that the Coast Salish always ate Bracken rhizomes immediately, because they did not keep well, but according to Duff (1952), the Halq'emeylem in the Fraser Valley used to store them.

The Straits Salish made a type of bread by pounding the roasted rhizomes into flour, mixing this with water, and forming the dough into flat cakes, which were then roasted. But this may be a relatively recent practice, since the Salish name for these cakes is the same as the Chinook word for bread or flour.

Bracken Fern patches were often "owned" by individuals or families, especially among the Vancouver Island Salish.

You can learn more about the use of Bracken Fern as a food in Helen Norton's paper (1979a in Additional References).

Warning

Bracken leaves and hay contaminated with Bracken are known to be poisonous to livestock when eaten in large amounts. The toxic ingredient is an enzyme, thiaminase, which destroys the animals' thiamine reserves. Judging from the widespread use of Bracken rhizomes and fiddleheads as food, this enzyme is not present in significant quantities in these parts of the plant. But there is more recent evidence that Bracken fronds are cancer-causing. For more information on the toxic qualities of Bracken, read the entry in Turner and Szczawinski's *Common Poisonous Plants and Mushrooms of North America* (1991).

CONIFERS
(included in Gymnospermae)

Sitka Spruce   *Picea sitchensis* **(Bong.) Carr.**
(Pine Family)   **(Pinaceae)**

Botanical Description
Sitka Spruce is a large tree, up to 70 metres tall, and 2 metres or more

in diameter. The bark is thin, silvery-grey or brownish, with characteristic long deciduous scales about 5 cm across. The needles are sharp-pointed, stiff, diamond-shaped in cross-section, about 2 cm long, and tend to project from all sides of the twigs. The cones hang down from the branches; they are about 6 cm long and cylindrical, with pale brown, papery scales.

Habitat: humid west coast forests, from sea-level to about 600 metres elevation.

Distribution in British Columbia: confined to a coastal strip 80 km wide; especially common on Haida Gwaii and on the west coast of Vancouver Island.

Aboriginal Use
The Haida, Tsimshian and Alaskan Tlingit used to scrape off the slimy cambium and secondary phloem tissue between the wood and the bark of Sitka Spruce, usually in late spring, and eat it fresh or dry it in cakes for winter. Often they mixed it with berries such as High-bush Cranberries before drying it. The Haida profess to have learned

about eating Spruce cambium from the Tsimshian comparatively recently, and say that some Tsimshian people still eat it today. The Nuxalk ate the cambium in the summer, but only as a laxative. The Haida and Kwakwaka'wakw, and the Makah and Quinault in Washington, used to harden Spruce pitch in cold water and chew it for pleasure, like chewing gum. The Makah in Washington used to eat young Spruce shoots raw, but there are no records for such a use by British Columbia First Peoples. Apparently, the Nuu-chah-nulth sometimes tied the boughs on submerged wooden fences to catch herring spawn (See Giant Kelp and Western Hemlock), but they peeled off the spawn after drying and did not eat the Spruce needles.

Western Hemlock (Pine Family)

Tsuga heterophylla (Raf.) Sarg. (Pinaceae)

Botanical Description

An evergreen tree, Western Hemlock is 30 to 50 metres tall and about 1 metre in diameter. The crown is narrow, and the top and branches droop, especially in young trees. The bark is thick and deeply furrowed in older trees, dark brown to reddish-brown. The needles are unequal in length, varying between 8 and 20 mm, flattened, blunt, white beneath in two bands, and usually spread at right angles to the twigs so that the branches are flat. The cones are numerous, about 2 cm long, annual, purplish to green when young and light brown when ripe, opening widely at maturity.

Habitat: humid to very humid climates; its shade tolerance is one of the highest among trees in this region.

Distribution in British Columbia: common along the entire coast to moderate elevations in the mountains, where it is replaced by the Mountain Hemlock (*T. mertensiana*) belt, west of the Rocky Mountains, as far north as the Parsnip River.

Aboriginal Use

Several coastal groups, including Haida, Tsimshian, Nuxalk, Kwakwaka'wakw and some Vancouver Island Coast Salish, ate the slimy cambium and secondary phloem tissue of Western Hemlock. A detailed description of the collection and preparation of this substance is given by Margaret Siwallace of Bella Coola, as told to Dorothy Kennedy of the B.C. Indian Language Project:

Long ago, the people helped each other store food away for the winter. If a person planned to give a large potlatch during the winter, he asked his friends to help him gather and prepare the food in the summer. They all went into the valleys to gather hemlock bark and camped there while they worked.

The men climbed the trees, using a rope around the tree to hold them. While they cut the bark, they sat on a seat. Using a sharp stick, called *iuta*, they sliced the bark from the tree and threw it down to the women, who then scraped the inner bark into little baskets. When the small baskets were full, they emptied them into a larger basket. All day they worked at this.

A deep, wide pit was dug in the ground and a fire started in it. The wood was crossed one over another and rocks placed on top. Then more wood was added. As the fire burned, the rocks became red hot. They pushed the chunks of wood to the outside of the pit and mixed the remaining charcoals with the rocks.

Meanwhile, the women gathered Skunk Cabbage leaves and spread them thickly over the rocks and sides of the pit. Next, the Hemlock bark was dumped over the leaves, using a long pole, with a blunt end, to push it into the centre. Then the bark was covered with more Skunk Cabbage leaves and woven cedar-bark mats. This kept the heat in as much as possible. A small hole was made in the top where water could be poured in. When it began to boil, the hole was covered.

The hemlock bark was boiled all night. In the morning, the cover was removed. The women readied themselves to pound the bark with their rock hammers. Their anvil was a large flat rock. The men removed the boiled bark, placed it in small baskets and gave it to the women. Beside every woman were two small baskets – one empty and the other full. When she finished pounding the bark, she moulded it into a ball and placed it in the empty basket. The people who were not pounding placed the baskets on racks, which were about 4 feet (129 cm) long and 2 feet (60 cm) wide. They were made from split cedar which was about 1 inch (3 cm) thick. The planks were tied at one end by cedar bark rope. Under the racks there were four or five pieces of wood so that the rack did not sag in the middle.

When the loaves of bark were on the rack, they were covered with washed Skunk Cabbage leaves. About four or five squares of bark were placed on one rack to dry in the sun. Then they were placed on a large rack, supported by two posts on each end and two in the middle, which held three or four small racks. They were lined up one next to another. When one side of the bark dried, the leaves were removed and the bark cakes turned over. After they were dried, they were stored for winter.

One cake at a time was taken out and soaked in warm water. Then it was stirred into a pasty substance and mixed with Grease. It was eaten together with Coho Salmon skin.

The Haida often mixed Hemlock cambium with High-bush Cranberries; such cakes are frequently mentioned in Haida myths as a feast food of supernatural beings. The Tsimshian apparently ate Hemlock cambium cakes only in the late winter, after all the preserved salmon had been consumed. Hemlock cambium could also be eaten fresh.

Occasionally, some groups also ate the cambium of the Mountain Hemlock, a subalpine to timberline tree. According to Anderson (1925), some Coast Salish groups ate Lodgepole Pine (*Pinus contorta*) cambium, but it was more commonly eaten by the Salish and Athapaskan groups of the central and northern interior of the province.

Hemlock boughs were frequently used by middle and northern aboriginal groups to catch herring spawn. When enough spawn had accumulated, they gathered up the boughs and dried them, then scraped off the spawn. The origin of this practice is recounted in a Skidegate Haida myth, recorded by Swanton (1905). Here is a summary of the myth:

Raven went to the dance house of the Herring People, and when he opened the door to look at them dancing, his moustache was covered with herring spawn. This spawn tasted bad, and Raven became disgusted and threw his moustache away. It grew into a seaweed (called "Raven's Moustache" in Haida). Raven then pushed a hemlock bough into the house and drew it out. It was covered with thick, good-tasting spawn. This is why Hemlock boughs are used to collect herring spawn today, in preference to Raven's Moustache.

FLOWERING PLANTS
(Angiospermae)
MONOCOTYLEDONS

Wapato
(Water-Plantain Family)

Sagittaria latifolia Willd.
(Alismataceae)

Other Names: Arrow-head, Arrow-leaf, "Indian Swamp Potato".

Botanical Description
Wapato is an aquatic, herbaceous perennial, 15 to 90 cm tall. The leaves are basal, long-stemmed and generally shaped like an arrow-head. The flowers are white, in whorls on elongated, leafless stems. The petals and sepals are arranged in threes. The plants are rhizomatous, bearing egg-shaped tubers 4 to 5 cm long, which are light brown outside and whitish inside.

Habitat: wholly or partially submerged in water at the edges of lakes, ponds and streams, or in wet mud.

Distribution in British Columbia: suitable habitats in central and southwestern British Columbia; most common in the Fraser Valley, although the continuing decrease of wetlands there has made it more difficult to find; extremely rare on Vancouver Island. Another species, *S. cuneata*, occurs east of the Cascade Mountains.

Aboriginal Use
Wapato tubers were a major source of food for the Halq'emeylem of the Fraser Valley, especially the Katzie, who owned large patches of the plants on the west bank of the Pitt River (e.g., north of Sturgeon Slough and around Siwash Island), according to Suttles (1955). Families in the Katzie tribe also owned Wapato sites. They could establish claims for a season by clearing other growth from tracts of

land a hundred metres long in order to have better access to the tubers. By the following year the patches would have grown up again and become common property. A family claiming one of these tracts might camp beside it for a month or more while harvesting the tubers. They gathered the submerged roots in October and November either by canoe, leaning over and pulling up the plants, or more often, by wading

in and dislodging them with their feet, allowing them to float to the surface. Raw and unwashed, Wapato tubers would keep for several months. They were cooked by baking in hot ashes. Wayne Suttles estimates that before the potato was introduced, Wapato was the most important starch food in the Lower Mainland.

Wapato tubers are said to resemble the Irish potato in texture and appearance, but have a sweetish flavour reminiscent of chestnuts. They were widely traded by the Katzie to neighbouring Halq'emeylem tribes, to the Nlaka'pamux of the Fraser Canyon, and to the Squamish and Vancouver Island Salish. They were eaten extensively by the Chinook of the lower Columbia River, and they were a major article of commerce in that region also.

Skunk Cabbage

(Arum Family)

Lysichiton americanus Hultén & St John
(Araceae)

Other Name: Yellow Arum.

Botanical Description
Skunk Cabbage is a perennial herb, with thick, fleshy rootstocks and large, oval-shaped, clustered leaves, mostly 40 to 100 cm long, bright green and waxy. Flowers appear in early spring, consisting of a yellow sheath, up to 20 cm long, surrounding a club-like yellowish-green flower stalk. At maturity, the stalk breaks apart to reveal brown oval seeds embedded in a white pulpy tissue. The skunk-like odour of this

plant resembles that of the closely related *Symplocarpus foetidus* of eastern North America.

Habitat: swampy ground, especially black mucky soil, beneath Red Alder and conifers. It rarely flowers in dense shade.

Distribution in British Columbia: common in coastal forests from Vancouver Island to Alaska and east to the Columbia River, but not in arid or semi-arid areas.

Aboriginal Use

Skunk Cabbage was rarely eaten by coastal First Peoples in British Columbia; but in western Washington, the Quinault roasted and ate the leaf-stalks, the Cowlitz steamed and ate the flower-stalks sparingly, the Twana (Skokomish) ate the young leaves, and the Quileute and Lower Chinook ate the roots. None of these groups prized any part of the Skunk Cabbage highly. In British Columbia, the Pemberton Lillooet (an interior group) ate the roots; the central and northern Nuu-chah-nulth dug them in late fall, along with Bracken Fern rhizomes, and ate them after steaming. The Squamish also steamed and ate the roots, but only as a medicine. The Kwakwaka'wakw dried and powdered the leaves and used them as a thickening agent for boiled Stink Currants to help make berry cakes. The Haida considered the plants to be poisonous and recalled instances of children dying after eating the leaves; still, they mixed the leaves with salmon eggs as a preservative. The Lillooet people at Douglas Portage once ate the roots in small quantities, according to the notes of Dr C.F. Newcombe recorded at the turn of the century; the roots were "hot, like ginger".

Wherever Skunk Cabbage leaves were available, they were used as "Indian wax paper" for lining berry baskets, berry-drying racks and steaming pits. They apparently did not impart any unpleasant flavour to the food.

Warning

Skunk Cabbage, like many other members of the arum family, contains long, sharp crystals of calcium oxalate. If any part of a Skunk Cabbage is put into the mouth, the crystals can become embedded in the mucous membranes and provoke intense irritation and burning.

Prolonged cooking and storage eliminates these crystals, but the roots should never be eaten raw, and the mature leaves should not be eaten at all.

Arrow-grass
(Arrow-grass Family)

Triglochin maritimum L.
(Juncaginaceae)

Other Names: Salt-grass, Goose-tongue.

Botanical Description
Arrow-grass is a grass-like perennial with thick, often woody rhizomes. The stems are 30 to 100 cm long, leafless and bear a long terminal spike of small greenish flowers. Leaves are basal, sheathing, erect and succulent. Leafstalks and flower stems are white and fleshy near the ground.

Habitat: common in salt marshes and estuarine flats, and on muddy beaches, often in extensive patches.

Distribution in British Columbia: along the entire coast, from Vancouver Island to Alaska; also in alkali marshes of the dry interior.

Aboriginal Use
Several Coast Salish groups, including the Comox, Sechelt, Squamish and Straits Salish, relished the whitish leafstalk bases as a fresh vegetable (but not the bases of the flower stems). The Kwakwaka'wakw and Nuxalk did not recognize Arrow-grass as a food, but the leaf bases were eaten by the Kaigani Haida and Tlingit in Alaska. They are best collected in late spring, and only the fleshy white part is eaten; the green leaves are discarded. The edible portion has a mild, sweet taste, reminiscent of cucumber. Within living memory, the Haida in Alaska canned them for winter food. Apparently, they also ate the leaves of a similar plant, Seaside Plantain (*Plantago maritima*). The Squamish and Comox refer to the edible leafstalks of Arrow-

grass as the "female" plant and the flower-stalks as the "male" plant. According to the Comox people, the male plant, if eaten, would give one a headache.

Warning
Although the use of the leaf bases as food by First Peoples has been well documented, Kingsbury, in *Poisonous Plants of the United States and Canada* (1964) notes that the leaves can be highly toxic to livestock, due to a capacity to release hydrocyanic acid. The mature leaves and flower stems should never be eaten.

Nodding Onion	*Allium cernuum* **Roth**
Hooker's Onion	*A. acuminatum* **Hook.**
Other Wild Onions	*Allium* **spp.**
(Lily Family)	**(Liliaceae)**

Botanical Description
All these wild onions are herbaceous perennials, with a characteristic onion odour, round or elongated bulbs, grass-like leaves and small flowers clustered in an umbrella-like head. Nodding Onion has tapered, pink-coated, clustered bulbs; the leaves remain green during flowering; the flower stems are 10 to 50 cm long, with distinctly nodding flower heads. Hooker's Onion has small spherical bulbs with a brownish net-like outer skin, short leaves that wither before the flowers appear, and flower stems 10 to 30 cm long. The flowers of both species are pinkish to rose-purple, but other wild onions have white flowers. True onions can be distinguished from similar bulb-bearing

Nodding Onion flowers.

Hooker's Onion flowers.

plants such as Fool's Onion (*Brodiaea hyacinthina*) and the so-called "Poison Onion" (Death Camas) by their unmistakable onion smell.

Habitat: rocky crevices and sandy soil in open woods or exposed areas.

Distribution in British Columbia: generally throughout the province, except on Haida Gwaii. Nodding Onion is the most

Nodding Onion bulbs.

common species, ranging from the rocky Pacific coast to the dry interior, the Kootenays and the Cariboo. Hooker's Onion is restricted to the dry slopes of the southern coastal forests, especially on the Gulf Islands.

Aboriginal Use
Several coastal indigenous groups ate wild onions. The Straits Salish ate the fresh bulbs at Bamberton. The Cowichan, Sechelt, Squamish, Comox and Halq'emeylem of the Fraser Valley also ate the bulbs raw or steamed in pits. Among the Nuu-chah-nulth, only the Alberni people had ready access to wild onions; they regarded them as the "older brothers" of fern rhizomes. The Kwakwaka'wakw marked the growing plants in spring and came back in August

Hooker's Onion bulbs and seed-pods.

to dig the bulbs. They steamed them in pits lined with pine boughs, covered with lichens and alder boughs. The Nuxalk and probably the Tsimshian, ate the bulbs, but the Haida were familiar only with cultivated onions.

Warning
Onion bulbs may be confused with those of Death Camas (*Zigadenus venenosus*), discussed under Blue Camas and in Appendix 2. The safest distinction is the characteristic onion odour of wild onions.

Blue Camas

(Lily Family)

Camassia quamash (Pursh) Greene and *C. leichtlinii* (Baker) Wats.

(Liliaceae)

Other Names: Common Camas (*C. quamash*), Great Camas (*C. leichtlinii*); Sweet Camas, Edible Camas (either species).

Botanical Description
These species of camas are herbaceous perennials with large, glutinous bulbs, 1.5 to 3 cm thick and 2 to 4 cm long, covered by a membranous brown skin. The grass-like leaves are basal, 10 to 20 mm broad and 20 to 40 cm long. The flower stems are 30 to 50 cm long, bearing a loose terminal cluster of showy blue blossoms in late spring. Great Camas (*C. leichtlinii*) is generally larger and stouter than Common Camas (*C. quamash*) and blooms two to three weeks later.

Habitat: meadows and grassy bluffs in soil pockets on rock outcrops.

Distribution in British Columbia: both species are common on southeastern Vancouver Island and the Gulf Islands; Great Camas is restricted to the west side of the Cascade Mountains; Common Camas recurs in the Columbia Valley south of Castlegar and is common in parts of eastern Washington and Idaho.

Aboriginal Use
Camas bulbs were a staple article of diet for many indigenous groups of the northwestern United States and were also widely used in British Columbia in areas where they were obtainable. They were especially important to the Coast Salish of southern Vancouver Island, but were eaten to a lesser extent by the mainland Halq'emeylem, Squamish, Sechelt, Comox, Nuu-chah-nulth and Kwakwa̱ka'wakw. The Nuu-chah-nulth often traded for them in the Victoria area, and the Kwakwa̱ka'wakw obtained them from the Comox.

Methods of collection and preparation of the bulbs vary according to tradition, but most groups dug up the bulbs during or after flowering, between May and August, and steamed them in pits. Sometimes, the bulbs were stored in Cat-tail (*Typha latifolia*) bags, but apparently they did not keep well.

Among the Vancouver Island Coast Salish, aboriginal harvesting and crop maintenance practices for camas can be termed semi-agricultural. Large areas around Victoria, such as the grasslands of Beacon Hill Park, and the small islands off the Saanich Peninsula, were frequented each year by the Saanich and Songhees peoples. They divided the camas beds into individually owned plots, passed from generation to generation. Each season, the families cleared their plots of stones, weeds and brush, often by controlled burning. Harvesting took several days, with entire families participating. The harvesters systematically lifted out the soil in small sections, removed the larger bulbs and replaced the sod. Even in this century, families would collect four to five potato-sacks full at a time. Most of these would be used for a communal feast upon returning to the villages.

Blue Camas bulbs.

They cooked the bulbs in steaming pits usually 1 to 2 metres across and almost a metre deep. The cooks lit a fire in the bottom and allowed it to burn until the rocks lining the pit were red hot. After removing the ashes, they levelled the bottom of the pit and placed seaweed, blackberry and Salal branches, fern fronds or Grand Fir boughs in the pit. Then they added the camas bulbs — as much as 50 kg at a time. Sometimes they mixed them with Red Alder or Arbutus bark to give the bulbs a reddish colour. Finally, they covered the pit with more branches, then with soil or sand and old mats or sacking. Water was poured in through a hole made with a stick, and the bulbs were allowed to steam for a day and a half.

When cooked, Blue Camas bulbs are soft, brownish and sweet. They were often used to sweeten other foods, such as Soapberries, in the days before sugar was available.

Contrary to popular belief, the bulbs do not contain starch, but a complex sugar known as inulin – the same substance found in the roots of the Spring Sunflower (*Balsamorhiza sagittata*) and Jerusalem Artichoke (*Helianthus tuberosus*). Slow cooking promotes the conversion of inulin to its component units of fructose, a sweet, digestible sugar. This is why cooked camas bulbs taste sweet.

Warning
Care must be taken never to confuse the bulbs of the Blue Camas with those of the closely related Death Camas (*Zigadenus venenosus*). The bulbs are similar in size and shape, as can be seen in the photograph. Death Camas has cream-coloured flowers that are smaller and in a tighter cluster than those of the two Blue Camas species. Death Camas commonly grows together with Blue Camas, and the leaves are difficult to distinguish. Anyone wishing to sample Blue Camas bulbs should dig them up at flowering time to avoid any possibility of misidentification. Death Camas is discussed in Appendix 2.

Pink Fawn Lily   *Erythronium revolutum* Smith
(Lily Family)   (Liliaceae)

Other Name: Pink Easter Lily.

Botanical Description
Pink Fawn Lily is a herbaceous perennial with elongated bulbs attached to small corms, and one or two brown-mottled basal leaves,

15 to 20 cm long and about 3 cm wide, tapering at both ends. The leafless stems are 12 to 35 cm long, usually bearing a single large, nodding, rose-pink flower. The petals are strongly recurved at maturity. The seed capsules are oblong, 3 to 4 cm long.

Habitat: forest openings and grassy places in fine sandy soil.

Distribution in British Columbia: on the south coast, notably Vancouver Island and coastal mainland valleys around Kingcome Inlet.

Aboriginal Use

Only the Kwakwaka'wakw and possibly the Nuu-chah-nulth ate the bulbs of the Pink Fawn Lily. The Kwakwaka'wakw dug them with special yew-wood spades when the leaves first sprouted in the spring. They stored the bulbs in ventilated baskets in a cool place. Some Kwakwaka'wakw people liked to eat them raw on a hot day, because the bulbs were cool and moist inside. Raw bulbs have a slightly bitter, milky taste. Another way of preparing them – for a feast – was to steam them in tall cedar boxes and serve them with large quantities of Grease. They could also be dried in the sun, then boiled in water until they broke in pieces, and mixed with Grease for serving. Or, for a simple family meal, the bulbs were baked for a short time in hot ashes and dipped in Grease with the fingers. One always drank water after eating Pink Fawn Lily bulbs; otherwise, it was said, one would get sick.

The above information was obtained from Franz Boas's *Ethnology of the Kwakiutl* (1921). Present-day Kwakwaka'wakw people no longer remember details of the use of this plant. Since Boas refers only to *Erythronium*, there is a possibility that the species involved was the Yellow Avalanche Lily (*E. grandiflorum*), a species widely used as food by interior peoples. However, Boas's description of the habitat (on river banks) would seem to be more appropriate for *E. revolutum*. Perhaps both species were used. Interestingly, the White Fawn Lily or Easter Lily (*Erythronium oreganum*), which is common in the Victoria area, seems to have been scarcely recognized by the Coast Salish.

Warning

According to Kingsbury (1964), *Erythronium oregonum* corms were incriminated in the poisoning of poultry in Vancouver. Their edibility should be considered doubtful.

Rice Root   *Fritillaria camschatcensis* (L.) Ker-Gawl.
(Lily Family)   (Liliaceae)

Other Names: Northern Rice Root, Mission Bells, "Indian Rice", Black Lily, Chocolate Lily (see following species).

Botanical Description
Rice Root is a tall, herbaceous perennial, with a large white bulb covered with rice-like bulblets. The stems are 25 to 50 cm long, stout and

have two or three whorls of narrow, tapered leaves on their upper portion. Each stem has as many as seven flowers; they are dark green-bronze to purple-brown, nodding, slightly bell-shaped and up to 3 cm long; they have a disagreeable odour.

Habitat: moist, open areas, from salt marshes to mountain meadows above 600 metres.

Distribution in British Columbia: common along the coast from Vancouver Island to Alaska and sporadic inland up the Skeena and Bulkley valleys.

Aboriginal Use
All coastal First Peoples harvested and ate the rice-like bulbs of Rice Root, except perhaps the Coast Salish of Vancouver Island and the Lower Mainland, in the Coastal Douglas-fir Zone, who ate the bulbs of the related Chocolate Lily. In most areas, the bulbs have not been eaten for 50 years or more; only the oldest people remember their use today.

   The Kwakwaka'wakw dug them with a yew-wood spade, spread them out to dry in the sun for about a week, then stored them in cedar boxes, covered with their own leaves, in a cool corner of the house. It was traditional for the owner of the bulbs to give a special feast to the Sparrow Secret Society during the winter dance season. The hosts of the feast steamed the bulbs for about half an hour in baskets set in tall cedar boxes. Then they poured Grease over them and served them to their guests, who ate them with spoons. They drank only a small amount of water after such a feast. For ordinary use, the bulbs were boiled a short time, then mashed. They never baked Rice Root Bulbs in ashes.

The Nuxalk dug them in spring, boiled them and ate them with sugar and Grease. The Haida dug them in July, usually along the sea coast. They boiled them in water and ate them as a thin paste, or in soft pieces, "like cauliflower", or they roasted them in embers and ate them with Grease. Older Haidas recall that bulbs from some localities taste better than others. Those growing near the beach, which are periodically covered with salt water, are the best tasting. The bulbs have a tendency to be bitter, even after cooking; the Tsimshian name for them means "to be bitter". In Haida, commercial rice is called "*Fritillaria*-teeth", after the little bulblets around the main bulb of Rice Root.

Rice Root bulbs and seeds.

Chocolate Lily
(Lily Family)

Fritillaria lanceolata Pursh
(Liliaceae)

Other Names: Rice Root, "Indian Rice".

Botanical Description
Chocolate Lily is a herbaceous perennial with a white bell-shaped bulb covered with rice-like bulblets. The stems are single, slender, 20 to 50 cm tall, with about two whorls of narrow, tapering leaves, fewer than *Fritillaria camschatcensis*. The flowers are borne singly or in loose clusters of two or three, nodding, bell-shaped and usually larger than *F. camschatcensis* flowers. They are choco-

late brown to dark purple and mottled with greenish-yellow specks. The seed capsules are upright, angled and winged vertically.

Habitat: meadows and grassy bluffs, often in association with Blue Camas.

Distribution in British Columbia: in the southwest from the Okanagan Valley to the lower Fraser Valley, and on southeastern Vancouver Island and the Gulf Islands.

Aboriginal Use
Chocolate Lily bulbs seem to have had the same dietary role for the Coast Salish of the south coast of British Columbia as *F. camschatcensis*

had for the middle and northern groups. The Squamish, Sechelt, Halq'emeylem and Straits Salish used them. They steamed the bulbs in pits or, when metal pots were introduced, boiled them. They are said to be tender and delicate, resembling real rice, except for having a slightly bitter taste.

Tiger Lily
(Lily Family)

Lilium columbianum Hanson
(Liliaceae)

Other Name: Columbia Lily.

Botanical Description
A tall perennial, Tiger Lily has an oval-shaped white bulb, up to 5 cm in diameter, covered by thick scales. The stem is slender, up to 1 metre tall, with many whorls of narrow lance-shaped leaves. The flowers are terminal, single to several, with bright orange recurved petals, dark-spotted near the centre. The seed capsules are oblong and tapered near the base. *Lilium columbianum* is also known as *L. parviflorum*.

Habitat: damp, open woods and meadows, from sea-level to sub-alpine elevations.

Distribution in British Columbia: throughout the province, south of latitude 54°.

Aboriginal Use
The Nuu-chah-nulth and Coast Salish, especially the Sechelt, Halq'emeylem and Straits Salish, ate the bulbs or "spuds" where they were obtainable. The Skagit and Clallam in Washington also ate them. The bulbs were dug at various times of the year, from blooming time in summer to late fall. They were cooked by steaming. They are said to taste like bitter roasted chestnuts.

Tiger Lily bulbs.

Wild Lily-of-the-valley

(Lily Family)

Maianthemum dilatatum (Wood) Nels. & MacBr.

(Liliaceae)

Other Name: Two-leaved Solomon's Seal.

Botanical Description
Wild Lily-of-the-valley is a low perennial with slender, branching rhizomes. The stems are 10 to 25 cm tall, usually bearing one leaf near the base and two near the top. The leaves are smooth, broad and

heart-shaped. The small, white flowers are borne in a terminal cluster. The fruits are round berries about the size of small peas. Before they ripen, they are hard and light green, mottled with brown; at maturity they are soft and red.

Habitat: moist, shaded woods and swampy areas.

Distribution in British Columbia: common in coastal forests, from Vancouver Island to Alaska, extending into east central British Columbia. Some botanists consider the interior form a separate species, *M. canadense*.

Aboriginal Use
Several coastal indigenous groups ate the berries, including the Squamish, Kwakwaka'wakw, Nuxalk and Haida, but they were sel-

dom highly regarded as food. The Kwakwaka'wakw called them "frog-berries". They, the Squamish and Nuxalk never cooked them; hunters and berry pickers occasionally ate them on expeditions.

The Haida used them to a greater extent. Haida children sometimes ate the raw green berries from the plants. The usual method of preparation was to pick large quantities of green berries and store them in water until they were red and

Wild Lily-of-the-valley fruit.

soft. Another method, used by Massett people, was to dry the green berries in the sun, clean them, and boil them for a few minutes in cedar boiling boxes by lowering baskets of the berries directly into boiling water. The soft-boiled berries could then be mixed with other berries, such as Salal, and dried in cakes. In one Haida myth, a feast for supernatural beings included High-bush Cranberries, Wild Crabapples, Salal-berry cakes, lupine-root cakes, Wild Lily-of-the-valley berries and Grease.

False Solomon's Seal   *Smilacina racemosa* (L.) Desf.
Star-flowered Solomon's Seal   *S. stellata* (L.) Desf.
(Lily Family)   (Liliaceae)

Botanical Description
False Solomon's Seal is a tall perennial with a stout, fleshy rootstock and leafy, arching stems, usually growing in clumps. Broad, elliptical leaves alternate along the stem in two rows; they range from 5 to 15 cm in length, and are notably parallel-veined and clasping. The flowers, small and cream-coloured, are borne in a terminal cluster. Numerous small, seedy berries grow in tight clusters. When immature, they are mottled green and brown; when ripe, they are red. Star-flowered Solomon's Seal is similar in form, but generally smaller

False Solomon's Seal.

Star-flowered Solomon's Seal.

and more slender, with fewer leaves and flowers. It produces only two to eight berries per cluster, which are larger and, before ripening, are green with red stripes.

Habitat: damp woods and open places.

Distribution in British Columbia: generally throughout the province, although False Solomon's Seal is apparently restricted to south of latitude 56°; neither grows on Haida Gwaii.

Aboriginal Use
The berries of both species are edible, but not especially palatable. They were usually classed with Wild Lily-of-the-valley berries in quality and appearance. Kwakwaka'wakw hunters and berry-pickers ate the raw berries of False Solomon's Seal on occasion. The Nuxalk occasionally chewed the raw berries of Star-flowered Solomon's Seal, swallowing the juice and spitting out the skin and seeds, but did not eat those of False Solomon's Seal. Other coastal indigenous groups apparently did not use either type of berry.

Calypso **(Orchid Family)**	***Calypso bulbosa* (L.) Oakes** **(Orchidaceae)**

Other Names: False Lady's Slipper, Pink Slipper-orchid.

Botanical Description
Calypso is a delicate perennial with a globular white corm. Each plant produces a single dark-green, oval-shaped, pointed, basal leaf, usually late in the season. The solitary rose-purple flowers are borne in late spring on stems 10 to 25 cm tall.

Habitat: the cool, mossy forest floor.

Distribution in British Columbia: generally throughout the province, from sea level to 1,400 metres elevation.

Aboriginal Use

The Haida used the small corms of this plant. They boiled them and ate them like Rice Root. They named the corms "black-cod grease" because of their rich, butter-like quality. Young Haida girls wishing to increase their bust used to eat the corms raw when they found them in the woods. The Pemberton Lillooet, an interior group, also ate the corms.

Note

Although these beautiful orchids are common in the province, they can be quickly destroyed in any locality by excessive harvesting. Sampling the corms is not recommended, since it means destroying the entire plant.

Eelgrass	*Zostera marina* L.
(Eelgrass Family)	(Zosteraceae)

Botanical Description

Eelgrass is a grass-like marine perennial with long, bright green, ribbon-like leaves, about l cm wide. Short stems grow up from extensive, white rhizomes; they are light green to white, and branching. The flowers are inconspicuous, enclosed in the sheaths of the leaf bases.

Habitat: extensive beds in sand, just below the low-tide line, usually close to the open ocean.

Distribution in British Columbia: common along the coast from Vancouver Island to Alaska.

Aboriginal Use

Several coastal aboriginal groups, including Straits Salish, Nuu-chah-nulth, Kwakwaka'wakw and Haida, ate the crisp, sweet rhizomes and leaf-bases. According to contemporary consultants, Eelgrass was not used by the Halq'emeylem, Squamish, Sechelt, Comox or Nuxalk, although its edibility was recognized, at least in recent times. The Saanich placed the rhizomes in steaming pits to flavour deer, seal and porpoise meat. The Songhees formed them into cakes and dried them for winter food.

Among the Kwakwaka'wakw, uncooked rhizomes, stems and attached leaf-bases were a favourite feast food. They gathered the plants in canoes, by turning long hemlock poles until the Eelgrass leaves were wrapped around them, then pulled up the entire plants. After breaking off the green leaves, they washed and carried home the rhizomes and leaf-bases. Usually the entire tribe was invited to an Eelgrass feast. The pieces were spread on mats, and each person took four, plucking off the small roots and peeling off the outer leaves. They broke the four pieces to the same length, tied them together in a bundle with the leaves, dipped the bundle in Grease, and ate it with the fingers. Guests could not drink water after an Eelgrass feast, but they could take leftovers home to their wives. This feast was an important one, because the Kwakwaka'wakw believed Eelgrass to be the food of their mythical ancestors.

The Nuu-chah-nulth gathered and prepared Eelgrass in much the same way as the Kwakwaka'wakw. The Haida apparently preferred to eat it when it had herring spawn on it. In the Haida language, the name for Eelgrass (*t'anuu*) is also the name of a Haida village on the east coast of Moresby Island.

Two closely related marine plants, known as Surf-grass (*Phyllospadix scouleri*) and Sea-grass (*P. torreyi*), were also used as food by some aboriginal groups, including the Nuu-chah-nulth and the Kwakwaka'wakw. The entire plants, including the long, salty leaves, were formed into square cakes and dried for winter.

FLOWERING PLANTS
(Angiospermae)
DICOTYLEDONS

Broad-leaved Maple	*Acer macrophyllum* Pursh
(Maple Family)	(Aceraceae)

Other Names: Big-leaf Maple, Common Maple.

Botanical Description
Broad-leaved Maple is a large spreading tree, up to 30 metres tall. The bark on the young branches is greenish to reddish, and smooth; on the older branches and trunk, it is grey and furrowed. The leaves are large, 10 to 30 cm broad, and deeply five-lobed. The flowers emerge in early spring, growing in drooping yellow clusters. The winged seeds are relatively large, usually in twos. The trunk and limbs are frequently covered with thick layers of moss.

Habitat: moist, forested slopes and bottom lands at low elevations.

Distribution in British Columbia: common in lowland coastal forests in the southwestern part of the province.

Aboriginal Use
Broad-leaved Maple was not widely used as food, but the Saanich and Cowichan placed the leaves in steaming pits to flavour meat, and according to Barnett (1955), the Vancouver Island Salish ate the fresh

cambium in small quantities, although "it made one thin to eat too much". The cambium was constipating, so was eaten with oil. It was also occasionally dried in criss-cross strips for winter. The Nlaka'-pamux people at Spuzzum, near Yale in the Fraser Canyon, and possibly also the Upper Sto:lo, peeled and ate young maple shoots raw, and also boiled and ate the sprouts when they were about 3 cm tall. The leaves, like Skunk Cabbage leaves, were used as a base for drying berries.

Pacific Hemlock-parsley	*Conioselinum pacificum*
	(Wats.) Coult. & Rose
(Celery Family)	**(Apiaceae or Umbelliferae)**

Other Names: "Wild Carrot", "Indian Carrot".

Botanical Description
Pacific Hemlock-parsley is a smooth herbaceous perennial growing from a thick, fleshy taproot or root cluster. The leaves are fern-like, being finely dissected. They are broadly oval to triangular in outline,

 and two or three times dissected, with lobed or toothed leaflets and sheathing leafstalks. The numerous small, white flowers are arranged in dense clusters in single or compound umbels, typical of plants in this family. The fruits are oval, hairless and ribbed, with broad, thin wings at the edges.

Habitat: common on gravelly or sandy beaches, grassy bluffs and headlands, and tidal marshes, mostly along or near the coastline.

Distribution in British Columbia: along the entire coast; almost entirely restricted to coastal areas, seldom occurring inland.

Aboriginal Use
In a paper published in *Economic Botany* in 1993, Dr Brian Compton identified Pacific Hemlock-parsley as the "Indian Carrot" or "Wild

Carrot" of the North Wakashan peoples, and, by implication, of the Kwakw<u>a</u>ka'wakw, Nuxalk, Haida, and possibly Sechelt, Squamish, Halq'emeylem and other coastal groups. Previous identifications of "Wild Carrots" under earlier botanical synonyms of *Conioselinum* by ethnographers C.F. Newcombe and Franz Boas, and confirmation of the identification by contemporary North Wakashan elders led to Dr Compton's conclusions. In the 1975 edition of this book, I suggested that Spring Gold (*Lomatium utriculatum*) may have also been one of the species called "Wild Carrot" and eaten as a traditional root vegetable. But Compton's research indicates that Pacific Hemlock-parsley is more likley to be the "Wild Carrot" most commonly used by central and northern coastal people. Long ago, people dug up the carrot-like taproots in the spring, then cooked and ate them; but today, few aboriginal people recall details of their use.

Harvesters marked the Pacific Hemlock-parsley plants in the summer and then dug up the roots the following spring before the leaves had sprouted. They peeled back the turf with a digging-stick and removed the larger roots, leaving the smaller ones to grow. The Kwakw<u>a</u>ka'wakw usually cooked the roots in a basket placed in a steaming pit lined with dry Eelgrass and fern fronds. They steamed the roots for several hours, then dipped them in Grease and ate them, but only with the right hand. Traditionally, one was allowed to drink water after eating them. In more recent times, the roots were boiled in kettles, like domestic carrots.

Another species, also known as Wild Carrot (*Daucus pusillus*), has been suggested as a wild root vegetable of aboriginal peoples, but since it is an annual, with only a minute taproot, it seems unlikely that it was harvested. Its relative, *Daucus carota*, the forerunner of the garden carrot, is commonly found as a weed on the southern coast, but was introduced from Europe relatively recently.

Warning

See the note under Cow Parsnip about the dangers of confusing edible and poisonous species of the celery family. Also, it must be stated that very few people today have experienced eating Pacific Hemlock-parsley, so any experimentation, without the wisdom of first-hand experience about its harvesting and preparation, must be approached with extreme caution. Although some sources have described "Wild Carrots" as sweet and tasty, Boas (1921) reported that they have a strong taste and may cause diarrhoea.

Cow Parsnip
(Celery Family)

Heracleum lanatum Michx.
(Apiaceae or Umbelliferae)

Other Names: "Indian Celery", "Indian Rhubarb".

Botanical Description
A robust, hollow-stemmed perennial, Cow Parsnip grows 1 to 3 metres tall, from a stout taproot or root cluster. The leaves are broad and compound in three large segments (one terminal and two lateral), coarsely toothed and lobed. The flowers are small, white and numerous, arranged in large, flat-topped umbrella-like clusters. The leaf stems are conspicuously winged at the base. The plants have a pungent odour, especially when mature.

Habitat: moist, open areas, roadsides and meadows, from sea-level to above tree-line in the mountains, often in large patches.

Distribution in British Columbia: throughout the province.

Aboriginal Use
Virtually every aboriginal group in British Columbia used Cow Parsnip as a green vegetable. They peeled and ate raw – or occasion-

ally boiled – the young stalks and leaf stems before the flowers matured. The outer skin, actually considered to be poisonous by some groups, contains a chemical that sensitizes the skin to light, which can cause blistering of the lips. The stalks were often dipped in Grease, and recently, sugar. Despite the strong odour of the leaves and outer skin, the peeled young stems are mild and sweet, resembling celery in taste. Most coastal First Peoples call it Indian Celery and interior people call it Indian Rhubarb.

Warning

Several members of the celery family, including Water Hemlock (*Cicuta douglasii*) and Poison Hemlock (*Conium maculatum*), are violently poisonous, especially the former. These plants are more slender than the Cow Parsnip, with smaller flower heads and finely divided leaves. Still, it is possible to confuse these species with Cow Parsnip, especially for inexperienced observers. Cow Parsnip and its relatives must be handled extremely carefully, because they contain phototoxic compounds, which make the skin sensitive to ultraviolet light, and therefore, to sunlight. That is why the stalks must be peeled before being eaten, and, especially for light-skinned people, even brushing up against the hairs of the leaves, and then exposing the skin to sunlight can cause severe blistering and discoloration of the skin that may remain for weeks or even months. (See Turner and Szczawinski 1991 in Additional References.)

Wild Caraway *Perideridia gairdneri* (H. & A.) Mathias (Celery Family) (Apiaceae or Umbelliferae)

Other Name: Gairdner's Yampah.

Botanical Description
Wild Caraway is a slender, hairless perennial, 40 to 100 cm tall or more, with a single or bifurcated, spindle-shaped root, pinnately compound leaves and a loose white umbrella-like flower head. The leaves, which usually die back by flowering time, are often quite variable: sometimes the leaflets are narrow and grass-like in appearance; sometimes they are broader and lobed or coarsely serrated. The grass-like leaves, though pinnately compound, make this plant easy to overlook unless it is in full flower.

Habitat: dry to moist open woods and clearings, from low to middle elevations.

Distribution in British Columbia: generally throughout southern British Columbia; its populations are often scattered, but it may be common in some localities.

Aboriginal Use

Several different plants in the carrot family were eaten by coastal aboriginal peoples, and Wild Caraway is evidently one of these. It was an important food of Plateau and Great Basin aboriginal peoples, and was almost certainly eaten within its range on the Pacific coast, but few people today recognize it as a traditional food. It is apparently the root called "Wild Carrot" sought by the Saanich people at Bamberton, and by the Squamish at Point Grey, but there is still some uncertainty whether this, too, might be Pacific Hemlock-parsley.

Water Parsnip
(Celery Family)

Sium suave Walt.
(Apiaceae or Umbelliferae)

Botanical Description

A perennial herb, Water Parsnip is 50 to 120 cm tall, with stout, strongly ribbed stems and fibrous roots, often originating from the lower nodes of the stem. A cluster of long, fleshy roots resembling miniature parsnips grow at the base of the stem. The leaves are singly compound, with seven to thirteen narrow, finely toothed leaflets. The flowers are small and white, in dense umbrella-like heads.

Habitat: swampy places and shallow water around the edges of lakes and ponds.

Distribution in British Columbia: common throughout the province, in appropriate habitats, except on Haida Gwaii.

Aboriginal Use

According to Suttles (1955), the Katzie Sto:lo of the Fraser Valley ate Water Parsnip stems, but details of their preparation are not given.

The Nuxalk and several interior groups, such as the Carrier, Nlaka'-pamux and Shuswap, ate the long, fleshy roots, raw or cooked. They considered the tops to be poisonous, however, and were always careful to distinguish this plant from the Water Hemlock, which is discussed in Appendix 2.

Warning
Water Parsnip has been implicated in numerous cases of livestock poisoning, although, according to Kingsbury (1964), they are not entirely convincing. Judging from its use by coastal First Peoples, the roots and stems are not poisonous, but the flower-tops may be. Water Parsnip often grows with Water Hemlock (*Cicuta douglasii*), which is violently poisonous, and the danger of confusing these two species is serious indeed, since they closely resemble each other. The leaves of Water Hemlock are three times compound, while those of Water Parsnip are only once compound. Water Hemlock also has a distinctive chambered, turnip-like swelling at the base of the stem, which is lacking in Water Parsnip. If you are even slightly uncertain about the identification of Water Parsnip, you should leave it alone.

Sarsaparilla   *Aralia nudicaulis* L.
(Ginseng Family)   (Araliaceae)

Other Name: Wild Ginseng.

Botanical Description
Sarsaparilla is a perennial herb, with long, branching rhizomes. Single, broad, compound leaves are borne on tall stems that grow at intervals along the rhizome; the leaf segments are 5 to 12 cm long with saw-toothed edges. Inconspicuous greenish flower clusters grow next to the leaves on shorter stems. The flowers mature to small berries, at first whitish, then dark purple.

Habitat: moist, shaded forests.

Distribution in British Columbia: common in the Bella Coola River valley and throughout south-central British Columbia.

Aboriginal Use
The Nuxalk formerly made a refreshing beverage from the rhizomes. They boiled them in wooden boxes until the water was reddish-brown. In recent times, this "tea" was sweetened with sugar. It was also taken as a medicine for stomach pains.

Indian Thistle	*Cirsium brevistylum* Cronq.
(Aster Family)	**(Asteraceae or Compositae)**

Botanical Description
A robust native thistle, 90 to 250 cm tall, Indian Thistle is a biennial or short-lived perennial with a thick, carrot-like taproot. The first-year

leaves are in a basal rosette. The flowering stems grow in the second year; they are thick and succulent, leafy, sometimes branching, and bearing flower heads in loose terminal clusters. The leaves and flower-head bracts are spiny, the flowers purplish-red. Indian Thistle has larger flower heads than the introduced Canada Thistle (*C. arvense*), less deeply lobed leaves than the Scottish Thistle (*C. vulgare*) and less woolly flower heads than the montane Edible Thistle (*C. edule*).

Habitat: moist clearings and recently disturbed sites in valleys and moderate elevations in the mountains.

Distribution in British Columbia: throughout Vancouver Island and the Lower Mainland, on Haida Gwaii, where it was apparently introduced, and recurring in eastern British Columbia in the Monashee Mountains.

Aboriginal Use

The Saanich, Cowichan and possibly some other Vancouver Island groups peeled and ate the taproots raw or steamed. Interior peoples, such as the Nlaka'pamux, ate the roots of another thistle, *C. undulatum.*

Oregon Grape	*Mahonia aquifolium* **Pursh** *and M. nervosa* **Pursh**
(Barberry Family)	**(Berberidaceae)**

Other Names: Barberry, Mahonia; *M. aquifolium* is sometimes called Tall Oregon Grape or Tall Mahonia, and *M. nervosa* Dull-leaved Oregon Grape.

Botanical Description

The two species of Oregon Grape are low shrubs with leathery, holly-like compound leaves, elongated clusters of bright yellow flowers and long clusters of round, deep-blue berries having a greyish, waxy coating. The bark is light yellow-grey outside and bright yellow inside. *Mahonia aquifolium* is taller and has five to seven leaflets per leaf; the shorter *M. nervosa* has nine to fifteen leaflets. The two species are sometimes called *Berberis aquifolium* and *B. nervosa*, respectively.

Habitat

Mahonia aquifolium grows in open, dry, rocky areas, while *M. nervosa* prefers light to shaded coniferous forest.

Tall Oregon Grape (*Mahonia aquifolium*) flowers and fruits.

Distribution in British Columbia: *Mahonia aquifolium* occurs throughout the southern part of the province; *M. nervosa* is confined to the southern coastal forests west of the Cascade Mountains. Neither species is found on Haida Gwaii.

Aboriginal Use

The berries, although extremely sour, were eaten by several coastal aboriginal groups, including Straits Salish, Halq'emeylem, Squamish, Sechelt and Kwakwaka'wakw. They were eaten raw off the bushes, or were mashed, boiled and mixed with other types of berries, such as Salal or huckleberries, for drying. Nowadays, the berries are made into jellies and jams.

Red Alder	*Alnus rubra* **Bong.**
(Birch Family)	**(Betulaceae)**

Other Name: Oregon Alder.

Botanical Description

A rapidly growing deciduous tree, Red Alder can reach 25 metres tall. It has thin bark, greenish on younger trees, turning grey to whitish with maturity. The inner bark and fresh wood tend to turn deep red-orange on exposure to air. The leaves are bright green, oval-shaped,

 pointed and coarsely toothed. The flowers grow in clusters of separate sexes: long, pendulant male catkins and short, woody female cones. Both are green and resinous when immature. The male catkins are reddish when they ripen in early spring; ripe female cones are brown.

Habitat: moist woods, swampy areas and recently cleared ground.

Distribution in British Columbia: common in coastal forests west of the Cascades from Vancouver Island to Alaska; sporadic in the southern interior.

Aboriginal Use

The Sechelt, Comox, Straits Salish and some other Coast Salish groups ate the slimy cambium tissue, between the bark and the wood. They scraped it off and ate it fresh, usually with some type of oil, or dried it in cakes for winter use. More recently, the Sechelt mixed it with sugar. The Saanich sometimes placed Red Alder bark in steaming pits with camas bulbs to colour them red. The Saanich and the Swinomish in Washington ate Red Alder cambium, only during an incoming tide; it was said to be most succulent at that time.

Hazelnut
(Birch Family)

Corylus cornuta Marsh.
(Betulaceae)

Other Names: Wild Filbert, Cobnut.

Botanical Description

Hazelnut is a bushy shrub, usually 2 to 5 metres tall, spreading and profusely branching. The young twigs are woolly. The leaves are broadly oval-shaped, pointed and sharply toothed. The male flowers are long, yellowish catkins, ripening in early spring. The nuts are borne singly or in clusters of two or three at the ends of twigs. They are encased in long, tubular husks, which are light green and covered with stiff, prickly hairs. When ripe, the nuts resemble commercial filberts.

Habitat: from shady forests on the coast to open rocky areas in the interior.

Distribution in British Columbia: widespread throughout the southern part of the province from Vancouver Island to the Kootenays, and extending into the northern interior.

Aboriginal Use

The Vancouver Island Salish, Squamish, Halq'emeylem, Nuu-chah-nulth and Gitksan (an interior group) ate the nuts whenever they were available. They picked them in early autumn and stored them, allowing the nuts to ripen completely, then ate them raw. Hazelnuts are both flavourful and nutritious.

Blue Elderberry	*Sambucus cerulea* **Raf.**
(Honeysuckle Family)	**(Caprifoliaceae)**

Botanical Description

Blue Elderberry is a large bushy shrub, sometimes tree-like, 2 to 5 metres tall, with brittle, pith-filled branches and grey-brown bark. The leaves are large and pinnately compound, bearing five to nine pointed oval-shaped leaflets. The flowers, small and creamy-white, are crowded in large, flat-topped clusters. The berries are small and numerous, dark blue, but appearing powder-blue due to a whitish waxy coating. *Sambucus cerulea* is also called *S. glauca*.

Habitat: valley bottoms and open slopes from near sea-level to moderate elevations.

Blue Elderberry flowers (above) and fruit (right).

Distribution in British Columbia: sporadic on Vancouver Island from Comox south to Duncan and on the Gulf Islands; occasional in the Fraser Valley; and common in the southern interior in the Okanagan and Columbia valleys.

Aboriginal Use
The Coast Salish living in the limited range of Blue Elderberry ate the berries. They usually cooked them first, and sometimes mixed them with other berries for drying. Blue Elderberries have a pleasant flavour but are rather seedy.

Red Elderberry	*Sambucus racemosa* L.
(Honeysuckle Family)	**(Caprifoliaceae)**

Botanical Description
Red Elderberry is a tall, bushy shrub, similar in appearance to Blue Elderberry. The twigs are brittle and pithy. The leaves are compound, having five to seven leaflets, which are elliptical or lance-shaped, pointed and sharply toothed. The flowers are in pyramidal clusters, numerous and cream-coloured. The varieties of berries found in British Columbia are bright red, borne on dark-purple tree-like stem clusters, which break off at the base when the berries are ripe. *Sambucus racemosa* is also known as *S. pubens*.

Habitat: open, swampy areas, moist clearings and shaded forests, from sea-level to moderate elevations.

Distribution in British Columbia: widespread along the coast from Vancouver Island to Alaska, extending into the interior along some major river valleys, and recurring in the interior wet belt along the Columbia River.

Aboriginal Use
Contrary to the commonly held belief that Red Elderberries are poisonous, the fruit was widely used as food by coastal First Peoples. Even today, they are used in some areas, such as at Bella Coola. In fairness, it must be said that Red Elderberries were not generally regarded highly as food, and were frequently mixed with other types

of berries to make them more palatable. But some people really enjoy them.

Harvesting began in late July and August, depending on the locality. Gatherers pulled down the higher berry clusters with long, hooked poles. They broke off the cluster stems at the base to keep the entire cluster intact, then removed the stems before cooking. Red Elderberries could be steamed overnight in pits lined with Skunk Cabbage, the leaves bent up at the edges to hold the juice, or boiled in tall cedar boxes using red-hot stones.

The cooks ladled the hot berries into cedar frames set over warmed Skunk Cabbage leaves from which the mid-veins had been cut, then dried them on a rack over a small fire for about 24 hours. They tied the cakes in bundles and stored them in cedar boxes.

The Kwakwaka'wakw always ate Red Elderberry cakes at noon; they were said to give one a stomach ache if eaten in the morning. They often ate them at large feasts. They broke dried cakes into dishes, soaked the pieces in water and rubbed them against the side of the dish until they fell apart. The feasters poured Grease over the berries and ate them with spoons, swallowing the juice, and spitting out the skins and seeds. They always drank water afterwards to wash out the seeds. They often mixed the cakes, after soaking, with Salmonberry, Red Huckleberry or Salal-berry cakes.

Old Kwakwaka'wakw women used to steam, mash and suck bunches of unripe Red Elderberries dipped in Grease. They ate roasted salmon afterwards to keep from getting sick.

Comparatively recently, sugar was added to cooked elderberries, and nowadays they are made into jam, jelly or wine. Only the Saanich people on Vancouver Island consider them inedible.

Warning
Kingsbury (1964) notes that the bark, wood, leaves and roots of Red Elderberry are considered to be poisonous, and that eating the uncooked berries may produce nausea. However, there is no definite evidence of the toxicity of elderberries.

High-bush Cranberry
(Honeysuckle Family)

Viburnum edule (Michx.) Raf.
(Caprifoliaceae)

Other Name: Squashberry.

Botanical Description

A straggling shrub, High-bush Cranberry is 50 to 250 cm tall with smooth reddish bark, and leaves that are opposite and shallowly three-lobed or occasionally lobeless. The flowers grow in small, rounded clusters, and the berries are round, shiny and red to orange. When unripe, they are hard and extremely acidic; later, especially after a frost, they become soft and palatable, though tart. Each berry contains a large, flattened seed.

Habitat: moist woods, stream banks and scrubby swamps.

Distribution in British Columbia: throughout the province, except in the dry interior, from sea-level to subalpine forests.

Aboriginal Use

The central and northern aboriginal groups of the British Columbia coast ate the acidic berries in large quantities; Coast Salish groups, such as Sechelt, Squamish and Comox, also ate them when they were available. High-bush Cranberries are becoming increasingly difficult to obtain, especially on Haida Gwaii, where they are virtually extinct in large areas. Most groups picked them in late summer or early autumn just as the berries turned red and were still hard and sour. They put the berries in tall cedar boxes, uncooked or after steaming for a short time, covered them with warm water and left them for several months. During this time, the berries became soft and red. Before the water froze in winter, it was drained off; the berries were mixed with Grease and other types of berries and eaten with spoons.

The Kwakwaka'wakw also preserved them by steaming them for one or two days in pits lined with alder branches, fern fronds and Skunk Cabbage leaves, before mixing them with a whitish mixture of Grease and water. Only a family group (a husband and wife, their children and close relatives) would eat cranberries preserved in this manner. At feasts, the Kwakwa̲ka'wakw served mainly fresh, frost-ripened cranberries, picked in bunches with stems still attached. They dipped the bunches in Grease, and sucked the juice and edible portion, discarding the stems, skins and seeds.

High-bush Cranberries were considered a prestigious food; among the Haida, and probably among other groups as well, patches of High-bush Cranberry bushes were "owned" by certain high-class people in a village. Only these people were allowed to pick the fruit. Boxes of preserved High-bush Cranberries were a valuable trading and gift item. Ethnological accounts and recorded texts and myths make frequent mention of this use, particularly among the Haida and the Tsimshian. They are the most frequently mentioned plant food in Haida myths; they were associated with salmon, and were thought to have been the food of supernatural beings.

High-bush Cranberries are still enjoyed by many people today. The Nuxalk serve them at elder's feasts, and some people preserve them for winter by freezing or canning.

Bunchberry flowers and fruit.

Bunchberry
(Dogwood Family)

Cornus canadensis L.
(Cornaceae)

Other Names: Dwarf Dogwood, Pigeonberry.

Botanical Description
Bunchberry is a low perennial, 5 to 20 cm tall, with creeping rhizomes. The leaves are elliptical, 2 to 8 cm long, with prominent longitudinal veins; they form a terminal whorl in groups of five to seven. The "flowers" are like miniature dogwood flowers, consisting of four white petal-like bracts and a central cluster of small true flowers with tiny greenish-white petals. The true flowers produce a tight cluster of bright red-orange berries the size of small peas. When ripe, they are soft with a yellowish pulp and a hard central seed. A closely related species of the coast is *C. unalaschkensis*, which has purplish petals on its true flowers.

Habitat: commonly forms large mats in moist coniferous woods and logged-over areas, especially on rotten logs and stumps.

Distribution in British Columbia: throughout the moister regions, from sea-level to subalpine forests.

Aboriginal Use
Bunchberries, though slightly pulpy, are sweet and flavourful, and they are abundant and easy to collect in some areas. A number of coastal indigenous groups ate them, including Sechelt, Nuu-chah-nulth, Kwakwaka'wakw, Nuxalk, Haida and probably Tsimshian. Several aboriginal people recalled that they resemble Salal berries in taste; the Sechelt name for them means "the one that pretends to be Salal". Bunchberries were usually eaten raw in early autumn with Grease and, in recent times, with sugar. The Nuxalk considered them "really delicious", while the Haida thought they were inferior to other types of berries because of their hard central seed. The Haida sometimes steamed them and preserved them for winter in water and Grease.

Stonecrop
(Orpine Family)

Sedum divergens Wats.
(Crassulaceae)

Other Name: Sedum.

Botanical Description
Stonecrop is a mat-forming perennial with short vegetative stems covered with small, succulent, berry-like leaves. The flowering stems are more erect, 5 to 10 cm tall, also leafy, with flat-topped clusters of yellow flowers. The stems and leaves are frequently red, especially in exposed localities. This is not the species of stonecrop common on  the rock outcrops around Victoria – *S. spathulifolium*. The leaves of *S. divergens* are smaller and plumper. Two related species, *S. oreganum* and *S. integrifolium*, also occur along the coast in some localities and, evidently, were eaten on occasion by the Haida and other groups.

Habitat: rocky ledges, ridges and talus slopes, usually in the mountains, but also along rocky shorelines and bluffs.

Distribution in British Columbia: in the Coast and Cascade mountains, and also along the coastline in the central and northern part of the province; Haida Gwaii represents the northern limit of its distribution along the Pacific coast.

Aboriginal Use
The coastal aboriginal groups acquainted with this species of stonecrop regard the fleshy leaves more as berries than as foliage. The Kwakwaka'wakw call it "crow's strawberry", and the Nuxalk name is "strung salmon roe". Neither of these groups considered it to be edible, but the Haida used to relish the crisp leaves as a food. They collected the berry-like leaves from small islands and rocky headlands, and ate them raw. They also chewed them as a flavouring, after taking fish-grease laxative, to make the mouth taste good again. The Nisga'a of the Nass River valley also ate them.

Soapberry
(Oleaster Family)

Shepherdia canadensis (L.) Nutt.
(Elaeagnaceae)

Other Names: Russet Buffalo-berry, Soopolallie (Chinook jargon).

Botanical Description
A spreading to erect shrub, Soapberry is 1 to 4 metres tall, with smooth brownish-grey bark and oval-shaped leaves. The buds, young twigs and backs of the leaves are conspicuously dotted with coppery scurf. Inconspicuous male and female flowers grow on separate bushes. The berries are small, soft, orange-red and translucent; they have a strong, sour-bitter taste.

Habitat: dry open woods.

Distribution in British Columbia: throughout the province, except in humid coastal forests; not on Haida Gwaii, and uncommon on Vancouver Island.

Aboriginal Use
Soapberry has been – and continues to be – one of the most widely used fruits in British Columbia. In areas where it does not grow naturally aboriginal people traded for it with neighbouring groups. They did not eat the berries in the usual way, but made them into a favourite confection, commonly known as "Indian ice-cream". The method of preparing this treat is similar for all groups.

Soapberries are harvested in mid summer. The gatherers place a fruit-laden branch over a mat or tub and whack it sharply with a stick. This method enables them to collect large quantities in a relatively short time. The berries should never come in contact with grease or oil – they simply will not whip if allowed to touch the smallest amount; now, even plastic pails are rejected as containers since they are "greasy" to touch.

To whip up Indian ice-cream, place a generous handful of Soapberries in a container with an equal amount of water, then beat the mixture into a light frothy foam having the consistency of beaten egg-

Indian ice-cream made from
Soapberries.

whites and the colour of pale salmon flesh. In the old days, aboriginal people whipped the berries with the hands or with a bundle of inner cedar bark, a Salal branch or Thimbleberry leaves. They used sweet berries, Blue Camas bulbs or Western Hemlock cambium to sweeten it. Indian ice-cream is still popular today, but now egg-beaters are used and the whip is sweetened with a small amount of sugar ("too much spoils the flavour"). In the past, Soapberries were preserved by drying, individually or in cakes. Today they are canned or frozen.

Soapberry froth was traditionally eaten at feasts and family gatherings. Special dishes and wooden spoons were used to eat it and a party-like atmosphere prevailed at such times. Adults and children alike used to play with the foam, sipping it from the spoon, and even throwing it at each other and tipping bowls of it over each other's heads.

The Kwakwaka'wakw traditionally obtained Soapberries from the Nuxalk and Comox. The Sechelt traded for it with the Lillooet at Pemberton. The Skidegate Haida obtained it from the Tsimshian and the Massett Haida from the Alaskan Tlingit.

The taste of Soapberries, like that of beer or pickles, is acquired; few people enjoy Indian ice-cream the first time they sample it. Even the sweetened froth has a sour-bitter taste, and an inexperienced eater is usually bothered by the air from the whip accumulating in the stomach. But once you overcome your initial dislike for it, you may find it can be a novel and enjoyable treat.

Crowberry
(Crowberry Family)

Empetrum nigrum L.
(Empetraceae)

Botanical Description
Crowberry is a low, spreading evergreen shrub, up to 30 cm high. The leaves are dark green and needle-like, giving the plant the appearance of a miniature fir tree. The flowers are pinkish and inconspicuous; the berries are purplish or black and grow singly along the stem or in clusters of two to five. They are juicy, but have large hard seeds.

Habitat: swamps, muskegs and rocky mountain slopes.

Distribution in British Columbia: in suitable habitats throughout the province.

Aboriginal Use
Crowberries have been widely used as food in the Arctic, especially by Inuit peoples. The Haida and Tsimshian ate them fresh, but only in small quantities. The Haida believed that eating too many would cause haemorrhaging. The berries are juicy, but the flavour is disagreeable to some people. Apparently, no other coastal indigenous groups in British Columbia harvested Crowberries.

Kinnikinnick   *Arctostaphylos uva-ursi* (L.) Spreng.
(Heather Family)   (Ericaceae)

Other Name: Bearberry.

Botanical Description
A low, trailing, evergreen shrub, Kinnikinnick forms dense mats, 5 to
15 cm tall. The bark is reddish and scaly. The leaves are thick,

oblong, rounded and tapered at
the base, 15 to 30 mm long, with
short stems. The flowers are
pink, urn-shaped and grow in
small clusters. The berries are
round and bright red; inside they
are white, dry and mealy, with
large seeds.

Habitat: dry slopes, sand and well-drained soils in exposed areas.

Distribution in British Columbia: widespread throughout the
province from sea-level to high elevations.

Aboriginal Use
Several coastal indigenous groups ate ripe Kinnikinnick berries,
despite their dry and mealy texture. These included the Nuu-chah-
nulth, Straits Salish, Halq'emeylem, Squamish, Sechelt, Comox,
Nuxalk, Tsimshian and Haida. The berries were usually soaked in
water, Grease, seal oil, or more recently, butter, to reduce the dryness
and prevent constipation. The Nuxalk formerly served Kinnikinnick
berries to chiefs at feasts; they dumped the berries into a large pot of
melted Mountain Goat grease and ate them with spoons. The Nuxalk
at Kimsquit dried them, then boiled and mixed them with boiled
"dumplings" made from flour and water. This was a favourite dish,
but obviously of recent origin, since flour is an introduced product.
   Coastal First Peoples also smoked Kinnikinnick leaves like tobacco. Before contact with Europeans, the Coast Salish of Vancouver
Island and the Lower Mainland, and the Nuxalk made special pipes
from hollowed-out gooseberry stems for this purpose. After contact,
the Haida, Tsimshian and Kwakw<u>aka</u>'wakw also smoked Kinnikin-

nick leaves, often mixing them with commercial tobacco; they must have learned of this use from the Salish within the last two centuries, since they had no knowledge of smoking before the arrival of Europeans. Once commercial tobacco was introduced, it was preferred to Kinnikinnick, although the latter was often mixed with it to make it last longer.

Salal
(Heather Family)

Gaultheria shallon Pursh
(Ericaceae)

Botanical Description

A creeping to erect, wire-stemmed shrub, Salal is usually 30 to 50 cm tall, but can reach 2 metres in humid conditions. The bark is greyish to reddish. The leaves are evergreen, tough and oval-shaped, with shallow saw-edges and pointed tips. Pinkish to white urn-shaped flowers grow in long, one-sided clusters. The berries are dark blue to black, hairy and fleshy, with numerous minute seeds, giving them a grainy texture.

Habitat: humid coastal forests and logged-over areas, often forming dense thickets; common on rotten logs and stumps.

Distribution in British Columbia: common on the coast up to 55° latitude, and as far east as the slopes of the Coast and Cascade mountains; also grows at Kootenay Lake in the interior wet belt.

Aboriginal Use
Salal berries are without doubt the most plentiful and widely used fruit on the coast. All coastal indigenous groups, from the Straits Salish to the Tsimshian, used them in large quantities. They picked them in clusters in late summer, and ate them fresh or dried them in cakes for winter. The Kwakwa̱ka'wakw ate the ripe berries at large

feasts; they dipped the berry clusters in Grease and ate the berries one at a time, then threw the stems in the fire.

The usual procedure for preparing the berries for winter storage was to mash them and either boil them in boxes using red hot rocks or allow them to stand for a day or two. The thickened "jam" was then poured into rectangular cedar frames set on Skunk Cabbage leaves and dried for a few hours on a rack over an alder-wood fire. The cakes were about 3 cm thick and could be as large as 30 cm wide by 90 cm long. The cooks folded or rolled the cakes and stored them in cedar boxes in a warm area of the house. Salal cakes were highly prized. The Kwakwaka'wakw would only use the pure cakes for a family meal or for chiefs at feasts. Cakes made to trade or sell and those given to commoners at feasts were usually mixed with currant or Red Elderberry cakes to make them last longer. Salal berries of poorer quality, or not yet ripe, were used in these "cheap" cakes.

To prepare the dried cakes for eating, the cook soaked them overnight in water, kneaded them until they broke into small pieces and mixed them with Grease. Feasters ate them with special black spoons made of Mountain Goat horn, which would not show the berry stains. Guests were not permitted to drink water after a Kwakwaka'wakw Salal feast. Salal berries were frequently used to sweeten other foods. The Haida used them to thicken salmon eggs.

Salal berries are still eaten today by aboriginal people, usually in jams and preserves. They apparently vary in taste and quality from area to area and some white people regard them as an inferior fruit because of their mealy or grainy texture. In my opinion, fully ripe Salal berries from robust healthy bushes are hard to beat for flavour and juiciness.

Labrador Tea
(Heather Family)

Ledum groenlandicum Oeder
(Ericaceae)

Other Names: Swamp Tea, Haida Tea, Hudson's Bay Tea.

Botanical Description

Labrador Tea is a scraggly shrub, 50 to 200 cm tall, forming dense patches. The leaves, crowded towards the tops of the twigs, are oblong with inrolled margins; they are densely fuzzy beneath. In older leaves, the blades are dark green to reddish, pointing groundward, and the fuzz is rust coloured. The flowers are white, in dense terminal clusters, and the seed capsules are brown and woody. *Ledum groenlandicum* is also called *L. palustre* ssp. *groenlandicum.*

Habitat: peat bogs, muskegs and wet mountain meadows, usually in association with Sphagnum moss.

Distribution in British Columbia: common throughout the province, in suitable habitats.

Aboriginal Use

Coastal First Peoples, like numerous aboriginal groups, European explorers and settlers across Canada, used the aromatic leaves of this shrub to make tea. Coastal aboriginal groups used – and still use – a variety of collection and preparation methods. The Haida picked the young leaves in spring, before the plants flowered, although leaves from the vegetative shoots could be harvested in summer. The Nuxalk and Comox, on the other hand, gathered the old reddish-brown leaves in late winter, just before the new leaves sprouted. They used the leaves fresh or dried them in the sun. Nowadays, they are dried in brown paper bags over a stove.

The Comox prepared them in a unique manner by steaming them in a shallow pit, in layers interspersed with Licorice Fern rhizomes to flavour the tea. They added water from time to time through a hollow tube at the top, and the leaves were allowed to cook until they were dark brown. Then they placed them in tall cedar boxes for storage (Bouchard 1973). To make tea, they placed a handful or so of leaves in a pot of water and boiled to taste. The Haida preferred a dark-coloured, strong-tasting tea, and often left a pot of it boiling on the stove for several days, adding more water as the liquid was depleted through use and evaporation.

Today, aboriginal people use plenty of sugar in it. You can make a pleasant beverage simply by steeping a small handful of Labrador Tea leaves in boiling water in a teapot, just as ordinary tea is made. This fragrant brew does not require sugar or cream. Coastal First Peoples, especially the Haida, also drank the tea as a medicine for colds and sore throats.

Possibly, some coastal aboriginal groups did not use Labrador Tea to make a beverage before Europeans reached the west coast. In many areas it is known as Hudson's Bay Tea and often, if an aboriginal name for it exists, it is of recent origin. For example, the Saanich know it only as Swamp Tea, and the Haida call it *xaaydaa tiigaa* (Haida Tea), an English borrowing. Perhaps the Hudson's Bay Company introduced the idea of using the leaves for tea rather than just as a medicine.

Warning
Two closely related shrubs, Glandular Labrador Tea (*Ledum glandulosum*) and Swamp Laurel (*Kalmia microphylla*), are known to be toxic in concentrated doses, and have killed livestock. These have a similar growth form and habitat to those of Labrador Tea (*L. groenlandicum*), but neither has the characteristic fuzz on the underside of the leaves. Also, Swamp Laurel has pink blossoms. Labrador Tea itself, while not harmful as a tea, is said by some to produce drowsiness or slight dizziness; but, to my knowledge, aboriginal people have never noted such an effect. Interior peoples also drink tea made from *Ledum glandulosum*, also known as Trapper's Tea, without any harmful effects; some say it is a good relaxant.

Alaska Blueberry (Heather Family)

Vaccinium alaskense Howell (Ericaceae)

Botanical Description

Alaska Blueberry is a deciduous shrub, up to 150 cm tall. Its bark is greyish on the older branches and yellow-green on the twigs. The leaves are oval to elliptical, pointed and smooth to finely toothed. The pinkish, urn-shaped flowers appear when the leaves are expanding, and are solitary and nodding with flared stalks. The berries, more erect, are bluish-black to reddish-black, with or without a waxy coating, and are rather acidic.

Habitat: moist coniferous forests and along shaded stream banks.

Distribution in British Columbia: mainly along the coast, but sporadic inland; particularly common on Vancouver Island and Haida Gwaii.

Aboriginal Use

Virtually all coastal aboriginal groups ate the Alaska Blueberries fresh or dried in cakes. The method for drying them was essentially similar to that used for Salal berries. The Upper Sto:lo dried them immediately after picking. They packed the mashed fruit in a 2-to-5-cm layer on a cedar bark mat and dried it about a metre above a fire for two or three days. Nowadays, the berries are canned or frozen.

Alaska Blueberries are not as sweet as Oval-leaved Blueberries; according to the Nuxalk, the Alaska variety is watery tasting. Both species often grow in the same area, but Oval-leaved Blueberries are distinguished by aboriginal peoples as bearing fruit earlier, which are greyer in colour and better tasting.

Mountain Bilberry

(Heather Family)

Vaccinium membranaceum Dougl. ex Hook.

(Ericaceae)

Other Names: Black Mountain Huckleberry, Black Huckleberry, Twin-leaved Huckleberry.

Botanical Description

Mountain Bilberry is a branching deciduous shrub with yellow-green twigs and greyish shredded bark on the older branches. It often

 grows low, but can reach 2 metres in height. The leaves are elliptical and pointed, with finely serrated edges; in autumn they turn bright orange-red. The flowers are single and creamy-pink. The berries are large, sweet-tasting, spherical and dark purple or black. Since they have no waxy coating, they are conspicuously shiny.

Habitat: mountain slopes and dry sites in coniferous forests.

Distribution in British Columbia: throughout the province, but rare on northern Vancouver Island and on the extreme north coast; not found on Haida Gwaii.

Aboriginal Use

Mountain Bilberry was – and continues to be – an extremely popular fruit among coastal First Peoples wherever it was available. Its Nuxalk name means simply "berry", indicating its distinctive status among types of fruits. The berries were gathered from mid summer to fall, and eaten fresh or dried in cakes. The Kwakwaka'wakw cooked them with salmon spawn.

Two other species of *Vaccinium* worthy of mentioning are Dwarf Clueberry (*V. caespitosum*) and Cascade Huckleberry (*V. deliciosum*), which would have been available to coastal First Peoples on occasion. Both have delicious fruits.

Canada Blueberry
(Heather Family)

Vaccinium myrtilloides Michx.
(Ericaceae)

Other Names: Velvet-leaf Blueberry, Sour-top Blueberry.

Botanical Description

Canada Blueberry is a low, deciduous shrub that grows up to 40 cm tall in dense patches. The leaves are oval to elliptical, thin, smooth-edged and velvety. The small flowers are greenish-white, tinged with pink, and grow in short, terminal clusters, expanding when the leaves are half grown. The medium-size berries are clustered, blue with a whitish waxy film, and sweet. A synonym for *Vaccinium myrtilloides* is *V. canadense*.

Habitat: dry muskeg, shaded woods and wooded rocky outcrops.

Distribution in British Columbia: mainly confined to the Kootenays and the central interior as a native plant, but also common in the lower Fraser River valley and delta area, where it was apparently introduced as a commercial crop plant.

Aboriginal Use

The Sto:lo along the lower Fraser River, picked these berries in large quantities. According to Duff (1952), the Upper Sto:lo used to burn over some patches each year to improve the yield. Other Coast Salish groups, including Squamish, Sechelt and Comox, acquired the berries through trade with their Sto:lo neighbours. An elderly Klahuse Comox woman related that, even before she was born (around 1890), a member of her tribe transplanted a bush of Canada Blueberry and one of Bog Blueberry (*V. uliginosum*) to a bog at Toba Inlet in Comox territory. These berries were still growing there in the 1970s.

According to descriptions, Canada Blueberries also grow sporadically in the Kimsquit and Bella Coola valleys, where they were harvested by the Nuxalk. Apparently, the Nuxalk also obtained them by trade from the interior Carrier and Tsilhqot'in peoples. Since the Canada Blueberry is the only deciduous blueberry with clustered fruits, its identification is fairly conclusive. The berries were popular because of the ease in harvesting them and their sweet flavour. Like other blueberries and huckleberries, they were eaten fresh or dried in cakes.

Oval-leaved Blueberry (Heather Family)   *Vaccinium ovalifolium* Smith (Ericaceae)

Other Names: Oval-leaved Bilberry, Grey Blueberry, Mouldy Blueberry.

Botanical Description
Oval-leaved Blueberry is a deciduous shrub, up to 150 cm tall, similar to the Alaska Blueberry in its form of growth and appearance. The leaves are thin, oval and rounded at the ends, with generally smooth margins. The flowers, appearing before the leaves mature, are solitary

and pinkish. The berries are of good size and flavour, dark blue, but usually covered with a waxy coating, giving them a grey or mouldy appearance.

Habitat: moist, coniferous forests and along shaded stream banks, and in drier woods in the interior.

Distribution in British Columbia: along the coast and in the interior, south of 56° latitude; very common on Vancouver Island, Haida Gwaii and the mainland coast, and in the Kootenays.

Aboriginal Use
Virtually all coastal aboriginal groups, except perhaps the Straits Salish on the Saanich Peninsula, ate Oval-leaved Blueberries; all regarded them highly. This blueberry is distinguished from the Alaska Blueberry by its slightly earlier fruiting-time, a greyer colour and a sweeter, more concentrated flavour. The berries ripen from mid July to September; they were eaten fresh or dried in cakes. The Comox used to mix them with Red Elderberries and Salal berries. When dried, Oval-leaved Blueberries taste like raisins.

Evergreen Huckleberry
(Heather Family)

Vaccinium ovatum Pursh
(Ericaceae)

Other Names: Shot Huckleberry, Black Winter Huckleberry.

Botanical Description

A thick, bushy evergreen shrub, Evergreen Huckleberry is usually 1 to 2 metres tall. The crowded, leathery leaves are shiny, oval, pointed and sharply serrated. The small flowers are white to pink, and grow in tight clusters. The late-ripening berries are small, black and shiny (or, occasionally, dusty blue), and have a sweet, slightly dry taste.

Habitat: gravelly or sandy soils in coniferous forests.

Distribution in British Columbia: almost entirely restricted to the southern portion of Vancouver Island, the Gulf Islands and the adjacent mainland; common in and around Pacific Rim National Park, and on Hornby Island and the Sechelt Peninsula; sporadic on other parts of the coast, but does not occur east of the Coast Mountains.

Aboriginal Use

The Nuu-chah-nulth and Sechelt, and some Vancouver Island Salish groups used Evergreen Huckleberries within their range. They harvested the berries in late autumn, usually in late October and early November. Undisturbed, the berries will remain on the bushes well into December, long after most edible fruits have rotted and fallen off. After other types of fresh food had disappeared, the women went out in parties to get these winter huckleberries. They are still eaten today.

Bog Cranberry   *Vaccinium oxycoccus* L.
(Heather Family)   (Ericaceae)

Other Names: Wild Cranberry, Moss Cranberry.

Botanical Description

Bog Cranberry is a slender, creeping, vine-like shrub with minute oval-shaped leaves spaced evenly along the trailing stem. The leaves  are dark green with a whitish underside. The flowers, growing singly on slender nodding stems, are deep pink with recurved petals and protruding stamens. The berries, round to somewhat elongated, remain hard and green well into autumn, usually turning red and softer after the first frost. In taste, they resemble commercial cranberries.

Habitat: restricted to muskegs and peat bogs, always in association with Sphagnum moss.

Distribution in British Columbia: in suitable habitats throughout the province. This species is treated by some botanists in a separate genus, *Oxycoccus*, and is differentiated into two species: *O. microcarpus* in the northern part of the province only, and *O. palustris* restricted to the central and southern parts.

Aboriginal Use

All coastal aboriginal groups in the province ate Bog Cranberries. Harvesters journeyed to the nearest peat bog or muskeg area in September and October, and picked large quantities of berries, still hard and mostly green. Most groups steam-cooked the berries until they were soft and red, or stored them raw in damp moss. Bog Cranberries were a common trading item between neighbouring groups. The Haida called them the "summer form" of the cranberry, and Low-bush Cranberry the "winter form", although both were harvested at the same time.

Wayne Suttles (1955) provides some interesting insights into the use of cranberries by the Katzie Sto:lo of the Fraser Valley. The most important area for harvesting them was a large muskeg near the mouth of the Alouette River. This region belonged to the whole Katzie tribe. Smaller patches, such as north of Sturgeon Slough and on Widgeon Creek, belonged to families in the tribe. Other Sto:lo groups travelled to the Katzie territory each year to pick the cranberries, but they always had to ask for permission from the owners before they could gather them. Permission was seldom refused, as long as the berries were not too green, and no payment was required, although the owners might then expect hospitality from the visitors later. Around the turn of the century, the Katzie and other groups used to sell cranberries to the settlers at New Westminster. If the berries were green, they would not bring a good price. Therefore, berries to be sold were picked later than those used traditionally.

At Ahousaht, just north of Tofino, there is a meadow where commercial cranberries were introduced as a crop fruit about 1920. They still grow there, and people still go to pick them in the fall. They are much larger than the wild type, but otherwise similar.

Red Huckleberry
(Heather Family)

Vaccinium parvifolium Smith
(Ericaceae)

Other Name: Red Bilberry.

Botanical Description
Red Huckleberry is an erect deciduous shrub up to 4 metres tall, with green, prominently angled branches. The mature leaves are thin, oval, smooth-edged and about 3 cm long. The young leaves remain on the branches over winter; they are dark green and serrated. The small, urn-shaped, pinkish flowers are borne singly along the stems. The berries are pink to red-orange, varying in size, but often 1 cm across. They are acidic, but of good flavour.

Habitat: shaded coniferous forests, often on rotten logs and stumps.

Distribution in British Columbia: abundant in coastal forests, from Vancouver Island to Alaska, but also occurring sporadically in the southeastern interior.

Aboriginal Use
Red Huckleberries were eaten by all coastal aboriginal groups in the province. They are still eaten in large quantities today in many areas. The berries ripen in mid to late summer. Often, harvesters would undertake long expeditions to pick them. When fully ripe, they can be harvested by shaking the berry-laden branches over a mat or blanket. Sometimes the harvesters used wooden combs to rake the berries off. Kwakwaka'wakw women cleaned the twigs and leaves off by rolling the picked berries down a slanted wet board into a basket; the leaves stuck to the board, while the berries rolled down. Some groups, such as Nuu-chah-nulth, preferred to eat them fresh. Other groups, including Sto:lo and Nuxalk, mashed and dried them in cakes, although they are quite juicy and had to be dried a long time.

The Kwakwaka'wakw boiled them in cedar boxes, mixed with red salmon spawn, covered them with heated Skunk Cabbage leaves, and sealed the tops with Eulachon fat (harder than Grease) and strips of heated Skunk Cabbage leaves. Prepared in this manner, the berries kept for many months. At winter feasts they ate them with the usual addition of Grease.

Nowadays, Red Huckleberries are canned, frozen or made into jam. The Nuxalk call red garden currants by the same name.

Bog Blueberry
(Heather Family)

Vaccinium uliginosum L.
(Ericaceae)

Other Names: Bog Bilberry, Bog Huckleberry, Sweet-berry, Whortleberry.

Botanical Description

Bog Blueberry is a low deciduous shrub growing up to 50 cm tall. It has many small branches that often spread out from the main stem. The leaves are small and bluish-green, smooth-edged, rounded and broadest at the tip. The flowers are small and pink. The berries are 6 to 8 mm across, dark blue with a waxy coating, and sweet.

Habitat: muskegs and peat bogs, associated with Sphagnum moss.

Distribution in British Columbia: abundant on the coast, particularly on Haida Gwaii, the southern coast and Vancouver Island, and in the northern interior of the province; not generally found in the central and southern interior.

Aboriginal Use

Several coastal aboriginal groups ate Bog Blueberries, wherever available, including Straits Salish, Halq'emeylem, Sechelt, Squamish, Nuu-chah-nulth, Kwakwaka'wakw, Haida and probably Tsimshian. The mainland Coast Salish picked them, along with Canada Blueberries, in the muskegs bordering the lower Fraser River. The Massett Haida obtained them in the extensive muskegs of eastern Graham Island, and called them by the same name as Saskatoon Berries: Sweet-berry. Bog Blueberries were eaten fresh or dried.

Low-bush Cranberry

(Heather Family)

Vaccinium vitis-idaea L. ssp. *minus* (Lodd.) Hultén

(Ericaceae)

Other Names: Mountain Cranberry, Rock Cranberry, Lingon Berry.

Botanical Description
Low-bush Cranberry is a low, evergreen, mat-forming shrub, up to 20 cm tall, with tufted branches. The leaves are small, leathery, shiny, oblong and rounded. The pinkish flowers are in short, terminal clusters. The berries are bright red, soft when ripe, up to 1 cm across, but usually smaller, and acidic.

Habitat: muskegs, peat bogs, rocky barrens and coniferous woods.

Distribution in British Columbia: sporadic on the southern coast and the southern Rocky Mountains; common on Haida Gwaii and throughout the northern part of the province.

Aboriginal Use
The Haida called them "dog-salmon eggs" and regarded them as the winter form of the Bog Cranberry. They gathered both cranberries at the same time, in October, and cooked Low-bush Cranberries a long time before eating them. They stored them in water in boxes, and later, in jars. Low-bush Cranberries have a pleasant flavour, somewhat like sour grapes, and leave a slightly bitter taste in the mouth. The Nuu-chah-nulth in the Hesquiat area may also have eaten them; some Nuu-chah-nulth ethnographies mention the use of several varieties of cranberry from Hesquiat Lake. The Tsimshian probably also ate Low-bush Cranberries. This species is widely used in Europe as a preserve.

Seashore Lupine
(Pea Family)

Lupinus littoralis Dougl. ex Lindl.
(Fabaceae or Leguminosae)

Other Names: Chinook Licorice, Beach Lupine.

Botanical Description
Seashore Lupine is a prostrate, mat-forming perennial with long rhizomes. Its leaves are typically lupine, palmately compound, with leaflets extending radially from a central stem. The plants are covered with silky white hairs, giving them a blue-green  appearance. The flowers are blue to purplish, pea-like and whorled in short, terminal clusters. The ripe seed pods, also pea-like, are black and hairy.

Habitat: a shoreline species restricted to sandy beaches and dunes.

Distribution in British Columbia: sandy shores on southeastern Vancouver Island and the adjacent mainland; recurring on the northeastern corner of Graham Island in Haida Gwaii.

Aboriginal Use
The Haida, Alaskan Tlingit and Lower Chinook at the mouth of the Columbia River roasted and ate the fleshy rhizomes, which are up to a metre long. The Kwakwa̱ka'wakw also ate lupine rhizomes, but probably Blue Lupines. The Haida dug up Seashore Lupine rhizomes at Tlell and Rose Spit in September. Sometimes, they roasted them slowly in the embers of a fire in which fish were being toasted; other times they steamed the rhizomes in pits dug in the sand and lined with Skunk Cabbage leaves. They peeled off the skin and ate them with Grease and, more recently, sugar. The inside is white and "as sweet as sugar", according to one source. For winter storage, the cooked rhizomes were pounded, moulded into cakes and dried.

Warning
Seashore Lupine rhizomes, like those of other *Lupinus* species, contain toxic alkaloids that can be harmful if the rhizomes are eaten raw,

although the Haida did not appear to recognize any poisonous qualities in the plant. The Kwakwa̲ka̲'wakw, on the other hand, ate lupine roots only in early spring and noted that they caused a drunken sleep when eaten raw (see Blue Lupine).

Blue Lupine   *Lupinus nootkatensis* Donn ex Sims
(Pea Family)   (Fabaceae or Leguminosae)

Other Name: Nootka Lupine.

Botanical Description
Blue Lupine is an erect branching perennial, 40 to 100 cm tall, growing in clumps. The leaves are numerous, radially or palmately compound, green and slightly hairy. The flowers are mainly blue and grow in long, terminal clusters. The seed pods are dark and hairy.

Habitat: a variety, from coastal bluffs to estuarine flats to alpine meadows.

Distribution in British Columbia: common along the coast from Vancouver Island to Alaska; extending into the interior in a few areas; a few isolated records from the northern Rocky Mountains.

Aboriginal Use
The Haida, Kwakwa̲ka̲'wakw and the Nuxalk at Kimsquit roasted and ate the rhizomes of Blue Lupine (although the Kwakwa̲ka̲'wakw may have been eating Seashore Lupine). The Haida and Nuxalk dug up the rhizomes in early spring, before the plants flowered, and roasted them in embers in the manner of Bracken Fern rhizomes. The Kwakwa̲ka̲'wakw gathered lupine rhizomes from Knight Inlet where the plants grow in clay soil on open river flats. They also collected

them in spring, "when the Salmonberries begin to have buds and the Eulachon first arrives . . . when the tribes are hungry," according to George Hunt in Boas (1921). They pried up the rhizomes with digging-sticks, washed them, and if they were really hungry, ate them raw. Eating raw lupine rhizomes can cause dizziness after a while. "When the woman and her husband eat too much of the lupine roots they become really drunk. Their eyes are heavy, and they cannot keep them open, and their bodies are like dead, and they are really sleepy. Then they go and lie down and sleep; and when they wake up they feel well again, because they are no longer drunk." This "drunken" state is caused by toxic alkaloids, mentioned in the Warning under Seashore Lupine.

Raw rhizomes were eaten only in times of famine. Ordinarily, the Kwakwaka'wakw steamed them by placing them on red-hot rocks in a cedar box or kettle, covering them with dried grass, pouring four clamshells full of water over them and allowing them to cook until the water boiled away. They dipped the cooked rhizomes in Grease and ate them with the fingers. They could drink water after a meal of lupine rhizomes. "Now they do not get drunk, and they do not get sleepy after eating [cooked] lupine roots."

Warning
Lupine rhizomes should always be cooked before eating. As mentioned above, lupine plants contain poisonous alkaloids that can cause "drunkenness" as described above. Under some circumstances, the poison can be fatal.

Springbank Clover
(Pea Family)

Trifolium wormskjoldii Lehm.
(Fabaceae or Leguminosae)

Other Names: Perennial Clover, Wild Clover.

Botanical Description
Springbank Clover is a tap-root, herbaceous perennial, with horizontal rhizomes up to 80 cm long, often forming extensive patches. The

leaves, like those of common lawn clover, consist of three leaflets joined at one point, but these are longer and narrower and sharply saw-toothed. The flower heads are pink to reddish-purple, often white-tipped, typically clover-like, but having a jagged green sheath at the base.

Habitat: restricted in British Columbia to coastal dunes, estuarine flats and tidal meadows where it is often a dominant species; commonly grows in association with Pacific Cinquefoil.

Distribution in British Columbia: strictly coastal from Vancouver Island to Alaska, but rare north of Tlell on Haida Gwaii; farther south its range extends inland to alpine meadow areas.

Aboriginal Use
Springbank Clover rhizomes were a highly important vegetable for a number of coastal aboriginal groups in British Columbia, including Straits Salish, Nuu-chah-nulth, Kwakwa̱ka'wakw, Nuxalk, Haisla and Haida. Just as the growing and harvesting of Blue Camas bulbs by the Straits Salish around Victoria can be termed semi-agricultural, the harvesting of Springbank Clover roots by the Kwakwa̱ka'wakw, Nuu-chah-nulth and Haida had characteristics akin to agriculture. They divided extensive patches of Clover growing along river flats into rectangular beds that were owned by families or individuals in a village group and passed from generation to generation. They did not actually farm the beds in the sense of sowing seeds, but they carefully removed larger rocks and sticks and only dug up the largest rhizomes, leaving the smaller ones to grow.

The Kwakwaka'wakw, Nuxalk and Haida dug the rhizomes in early spring or in the fall after the frost had killed the leaves. The Nuu-chah-nulth dug them in late summer. None of these groups ordinarily ate raw Clover rhizomes, except as a snack by the women digging them. The harvesters spread damp or muddy rhizomes on mats to dry for two days and then brushed off the dirt and sand. The dried rhizomes keep for a considerable period of time if stored in a cool place.

Various methods were employed to cook them. For a quick meal on camping expeditions, a Kwakwaka'wakw woman wrapped the cleaned rhizomes in Skunk Cabbage leaves and buried them in the hot ashes under the fire to roast. For ordinary family meals, she piled them on a cedar-wood grid in a kettle, covered them with damp cedar bark and boiled them. For a Kwakwaka'wakw feast, the cooks steamed Clover rhizomes in tall cedar boxes. The guests ate scorched dried salmon first, then the Clover roots with the fingers, dipping them in Grease in the usual manner. According to Kwakwaka'wakw etiquette, guests were required to finish all the Clover roots served to them; no leftovers were allowed.

The Saanich, Nuxalk and Haida steamed the rhizomes in pits and, more recently, in kettles, "like chow mein" (bean sprouts). They ate them with Grease and sugar. The Nuxalk sometimes ate them with "stink eggs" (fermented salmon roe). The Nuu-chah-nulth, rather than dig a steaming pit, sometimes heated a large pile of stones at ground-level by building a large fire over them, then covered them with successive layers of damp seaweed, Salmonberry leaves, Springbank Clover rhizomes, more seaweed, and so on, until all the Clover roots were on the pile. They piled old mats on top and, as the seaweed dried out, poured water into the pile through a channel left in the middle. Drucker (1951) refers to instances where young men had to climb to the roof of the house in order to pour in water, "so high were the piles of Clover roots".

Coastal First Peoples differentiate between two types of Clover roots – the long horizontal rhizomes that resemble spaghetti but are finer; and the short, gnarled, fleshy tap-roots. These are separated at digging-time and cooked in separate batches. The Kwakwaka'wakw reserved the long roots for chiefs and high-class families at feasts and left the short ones for commoners. The best Clover rhizomes are found in soft, sandy soil, where they are not bent and twisted by rocks.

For more information on this interesting plant, read the paper by Turner and Kuhnlein (1982), listed in Additional References.

Giant Vetch
(Pea Family)

Vicia gigantea Hook.
(Fabaceae or Leguminosae)

Botanical Description

A succulent, climbing herbaceous perennial, Giant Vetch grows 1 to 2 metres tall. It has soft, ridged green stems and compound leaves con-

 sisting of numerous (19 to 29) elongated leaflets, each 2 to 4 cm long, forming two rows along a central stem, which terminates in a well-developed tendril. The pea-like flowers are flesh-coloured to purplish, in clusters of 6 to 14. The pods, when ripe, are 2 to 5 cm long, resembling pea pods, but they are black and dry; each contains three or four round seeds the size of baby peas.

Habitat: commonly coastal, along the upper shoreline, but also occurs inland in moist forest clearings and roadsides.

Distribution in British Columbia: along the coastline from Vancouver Island to Alaska.

Aboriginal Use

Some aboriginal groups, such as the Saanich, considered the seeds of the Giant Vetch to be poisonous, and others regarded them with suspicion. But the Kwakwa̱ka'wakw ate them as a snack, roasting the green pods in an open fire, watching them carefully so they wouldn't burn. When the pods started to split open, they took them out, removed the seeds and ate them. They did not eat them in any quantity. Even the young seeds are strong tasting, like old garden peas.

Warning

Several species of vetch, including some in British Columbia, have been reported to be toxic to livestock and children. Giant Vetch itself has not been implicated, but be cautious eating the seeds.

Garry Oak
(Beech Family)

Quercus garryana Dougl. ex Hook.
(Fagaceae)

Botanical Description
Garry Oak is a spreading, deciduous tree, 10 to 25 metres tall,
with a thick trunk and grey, furrowed bark. The leaves are dark
green and shiny, with rounded
lobes. The female flowers are
inconspicuous and the male flowers are in thin, drooping catkins.
The fruits are light brown acorns,
about 2 cm long, with shallow cups.

Habitat: dry, open woods and on rock outcrops.

Distribution in British Columbia: southeastern Vancouver Island
and the Gulf Islands; rarely in the Fraser Valley; found nowhere else
in Canada.

Aboriginal Use
Some Vancouver Island Coast Salish groups, especially the Straits
Salish, ate the acorns; several aboriginal groups of western
Washington also ate them. The acorns, like those of all oaks, have a
high tannin content. Although they can be eaten raw, as they were by
the Washington Clallam, they are very bitter. The Vancouver Island
Salish preferred them steamed, roasted or boiled for a long time to
remove the bitterness. They did not, however, use the elaborate
methods for leaching acorns employed by some aboriginal groups in
Oregon and California, where acorns were a staple article of diet.

Warning
The buds, leaves and acorns of many species of oaks have been
reported in Kingsbury (1964) to be toxic to livestock, although acorns
are a common food of domestic swine. On the ranges of the southwestern United States, annual losses due to oak poisoning are in the
millions of dollars. Garry Oak is not directly implicated, but it should
be regarded with suspicion.

Stink Currant
(Gooseberry Family)

Ribes bracteosum Dougl. ex Hook.
(Grossulariaceae)

Other Names: Greyberry, Skunk Currant, Blue Currant.

Botanical Description

Stink Currant is an erect, scraggly shrub, without spines or prickles, growing 150 to 300 cm tall or even taller. It has greyish bark dotted with small, yellow crystalline glands. The leaves are large, resembling Thimbleberry or maple leaves, with 5 to 7 pointed, toothed lobes.

The plants emit a characteristic musky odour. The flowers are numerous, small and greenish to white, growing in long, erect clusters. The berries are rounded or elongated, and blue with a waxy coating, giving them a blue-grey appearance. They are spotted with dark glands. Their taste ranges from musky to bland but is generally not unpleasant.

Habitat: shaded stream banks and swamps in seepage areas, usually in black, mucky soil.

Distribution in British Columbia: west of the Cascade Mountains, from Vancouver Island to Alaska.

Aboriginal Use

Stink Currants were a common food of the coastal First Peoples. Some groups, such as the Nuxalk, favoured them as a fruit, while other groups, such as the Squamish, ate them only out of necessity. Stink Currant berries were picked in late summer. At this time, the Kwakwaka'wakw ate them raw at informal feasts, with spoons made from Mountain Goat horn. They ate large quantities of oil or Grease with them to avoid constipation. Chiefs and their wives ate them mashed with Salal berries. To preserve Stink Currants for winter, Kwakwaka'wakw cooks boiled them in tall cedar boxes, mixed them with powdered Skunk Cabbage leaves, and dried them for four or five days in wooden frames set over a fire. To eat the preserved berries at large feasts in winter, they soaked them in water until they dissolved, then mixed them with Grease. The guests had to eat all the currants in their dishes or they would have bad luck.

Stink Currants are still eaten occasionally in some areas; they are eaten fresh with milk and sugar, or made into jam.

Coastal Black Gooseberry (Gooseberry Family)

Ribes divaricatum Dougl. (Grossulariaceae)

Botanical Description

An erect to spreading deciduous shrub, Coastal Black Gooseberry is usually about 2 metres tall with arching branches and smooth greyish bark. The stems are not prickly but have one to three stout spines at each node. The leaves are small and shaped like a maple leaf with three to five main lobes. The flowers are small, red to reddish-green, with  recurving petal-like sepals, and are borne in drooping clusters of two to four. The berries are spherical and smooth, with a brown "wick" at the end. Unripe, they are grape-green; ripe, they are purplish-black with a translucent skin. They have a good flavour.

Habitat: open woods and moist clearings, particularly along the coastline.

Distribution in British Columbia: common west of the Cascade and Coast mountains, but also found in the Lillooet area; not on Haida Gwaii.

Aboriginal Use

All coastal aboriginal groups in the province, except the Haida, ate Coastal Black Gooseberries. The Kwakwa̱ka'wakw gathered them, full-size but still green, in mid summer. They gathered the berries by spreading a mat or blanket beneath the bushes and beating the branches with a stick. To separate the fruit from dead leaves and sticks, a woman would stand in the doorway in a strong wind and pour the berries onto a mat: the lighter material blew away. The Kwakw<u>aka</u>'wakw sometimes ate the berries raw and green, but for a feast they usually boiled them for a long time, cooled them, and ate them with Grease. They never drank water after a gooseberry feast.

In spring, when the berries were just beginning to ripen, the Nuxalk picked them green, along with the leaves, and boiled them together to make a thick sauce that was considered a delicacy. The Sechelt picked the berries green, but allowed them to ripen before eating them. All of the groups also picked and ate the berries when they were ripe and purple. They seldom dried them in cakes. Coastal Black Gooseberries are still eaten today, fresh with milk and sugar, canned, or made into jam and jelly. The berries are tart, especially when green, but have a delightful tangy flavour.

Swamp Gooseberry   *Ribes lacustre* (Pers.) Poir.
(Gooseberry Family)   (Grossulariaceae)

Other Names: Swamp Currant, Prickly Currant.

Botanical Description
Swamp Gooseberry is an erect to spreading deciduous shrub 1 to 2 metres tall, with light reddish-brown stems. The stems are usually thickly covered with thin, sharp, spines as well as having thicker

thorns at the nodes. The leaves are small and shaped like maple leaves, with sharp, deeply indented lobes. The flowers are small and disc-like, usually reddish, in drooping clusters of seven to fifteen. The berries, in clusters of three or four, are small, dark purple and covered with conspicuous bristles. When fully ripe, they have an agreeable flavour.

Habitat: moist, open woods and stream banks, often on rotten stumps and damp rocky cliffs, from sea-level to subalpine forest.

Distribution in British Columbia: common throughout the province.

Aboriginal Use
Most coastal aboriginal groups ate the berries, but the Sechelt considered them to be poisonous. Most people ate the berries fresh, right from the bushes; they are usually too small and difficult to collect to be used in any quantity. Both the Sechelt and Nuxalk regarded the spines as highly poisonous to touch, causing violent swelling, though the Nuxalk still ate the berries when they could pick them without touching the spines. Like those of Devil's Club, Swamp Gooseberry spines can produce a serious allergic reaction in some people.

White-flowered Currant (Gooseberry Family)

Ribes laxiflorum Pursh (Grossulariaceae)

Other Name: Wild Black Currant, Trailing Currant.

Botanical Description
A straggly, spreading, deciduous shrub, without prickles, White-flowered Currant is usually 1 to 2 metres tall, but taller in dense woods, or often hanging down from stumps and rock faces. The bark is reddish-brown and the leaves are like maple leaves with five sharp, coarsely toothed lobes, slightly broader than long and often

turning orange by late summer. The flowers are small, red and white, in long, erect clusters. The berries are purplish-black, with a waxy coating, up to 1 cm long but usually smaller, and finely covered with black bristles.

Habitat: wet coastal woods to montane slopes; especially prevalent on rock faces and rotten stumps in logged areas or clearings.

Distribution in British Columbia: mainly west of the Coast Mountains, from Alaska south, but also occurring in the Cariboo, and in the Selkirk and Rocky mountains.

Aboriginal Use

Several coastal aboriginal groups ate the berries, including the Nuxalk, Kwakwaka'wakw, Haida and Tsimshian, although not in large quantities and usually right from the bushes. White-flowered Currants are palatable but not very juicy. The Kwakwaka'wakw called them by the same name as Oregon Grape, presumably because they are similar in size and colour.

Sticky Gooseberry   *Ribes lobbii* Gray
(Gooseberry Family)   (Grossulariaceae)

Other Names: Red-flowered Gooseberry, Gummy Gooseberry.

Botanical Description

A stout, branching shrub usually under 1 metre tall, Sticky Gooseberry has reddish-grey bark and three sharp spines at each stem node. The leaves are small with three (or five) rounded lobes.

 The drooping flowers are single or in pairs; they are relatively large and showy, with bright red, recurving petal-like sepals and a white central tube of petals and stamens. The large, spherical or elongated berries are green when unripe and reddish-brown to purple when ripe; they are covered with sticky hairs.

Habitat: dry, open, well-drained woods and clearings.

Distribution in British Columbia: southeastern Vancouver Island, the Gulf Islands and the Lower Mainland west of the Cascade Mountains.

Aboriginal Use

The berries, though generally unpalatable, were eaten by the Kwakwaka'wakw and the Vancouver Island Salish, but only in small quantities.

Red-flowering Currant
(Gooseberry Family)

Ribes sanguineum Pursh
(Grossulariaceae)

Botanical Description

Red-flowering Currant is an erect, deciduous shrub that grows up to 3 (or more) metres tall, with reddish-brown to grey bark and no prickles. The leaves are maple-like, with five coarsely toothed, rounded lobes. The flowers, which bloom in early spring, are small and rose-pink to bright red; they grow in crowded, elongated, drooping clusters that are very conspicuous. The berries are round and dark blue, but with a waxy coating giving them a sky-blue colour. The plants have a distinctive aroma.

Habitat: dry open woods, logged areas and roadsides in well-drained soils.

Distribution in British Columbia: low elevations in the southwestern part of the province and sporadic in the Kootenays; common on southern Vancouver Island.

Aboriginal Use

The berries of Red-flowering Currant are edible but insipid. Various Coast Salish groups, such as the Saanich, Cowichan, Squamish and Sechelt, ate them fresh, but rarely dried them. They did not regard them highly. Some Cowichan children were taught that picking the flowers would cause rain.

Red-flowering Currant flowers and fruits.

Yerba Buena
(Mint Family)

Satureja douglasii (Benth.) Briq.
(Lamiaceae or Labiatae)

Botanical Description

Yerba Buena is a slender, trailing, herbaceous perennial with some short upright stems. The leaves, growing in pairs along the stem, are

thick, shiny, often purplish (especially underneath) and egg-shaped, bluntly pointed and slightly toothed. They emit a fragrant, savory odour when crushed. The flowers, borne in small groups at the stem nodes, are whitish and inconspicuous. *Satureja douglasii* is also known as *Micromeria douglasii.*

Habitat: dry woods and open fields, often spreading vegetatively.

Distribution in British Columbia: southern Vancouver Island, the Gulf Islands and the Lower Mainland west of the Cascades; recurring in the Kootenays.

Aboriginal Use

The Saanich, and possibly some other Straits Salish groups, made a refreshing tea by steeping the leaves of Yerba Buena in boiling water. They drank the tea as a beverage, but also considered it a good tonic. A small handful of leaves per cup of water gives a good flavour.

Purple Hedge Nettle
(Mint Family)

Stachys cooleyae Heller
(Lamiaceae or Labiatae)

Botanical Description

Purple Hedge Nettle is a tall, slender-stemmed, herbaceous perennial resembling Stinging Nettle in over-all form, but with conspicuously square stems and thinly fuzzy leaves. The leaves are opposite, coarsely toothed, pointed and narrowly heart-shaped, generally decreasing in size up the stem. The small, reddish-purple flowers grow in a long, terminal cluster. *Stachys cooleyae* is also called *S. ciliata*.

Habitat: forming small patches in shaded swamps, thickets and lowland depressions from sea-level to moderate elevations.

Distribution in British Columbia: west of the coastal mountains, from Vancouver Island to Haida Gwaii and Prince Rupert.

Aboriginal Use

The Haida, especially the children, used to chew the young stems of Purple Hedge Nettle, sucking out the juice and discarding the fibre. Other aboriginal groups did not consider it edible, although the Saanich made a spring tonic by steeping the crushed rhizomes in hot water.

Fireweed
(Evening Primrose Family)

Epilobium angustifolium L.
(Onagraceae)

Other Name: Willow Herb.

Botanical Description
Fireweed is a tall, smooth-stemmed, herbaceous perennial, with spreading rhizomes and alternate, smooth-edged, lance-shaped leaves resembling those of narrow-leaved willows. The flowers are red-pur-

ple with four petals; they grow in long, terminal clusters, and are very showy. They bloom throughout the summer, in sequence from bottom to top. The seed capsules are long and narrow, splitting longitudinally on all four sides to reveal rows of small parachuted seeds. The seeds can travel on the wind for long distances.

Habitat: extensive patches in open clearings, logged areas, burns and roadsides. In summer it often colours entire hillsides pink.

Distribution in British Columbia: widespread throughout the province.

Aboriginal Use
The inner part of the stem, especially in young plants, is sweet and succulent. A number of coastal aboriginal groups, including Sechelt, Squamish, Nuxalk, Haida and Tsimshian, ate Fireweed raw as a green vegetable. The Haida apparently used it more than other groups, gathering the tall stems in large quantities in spring and eating them at feasts. They split each shoot length-wise with the thumbnail and sprinkled it with sugar.

Edible shoots of Fireweed.

Then they pulled pieces several inches long through the teeth, scraping off the tender inner part, as in eating artichoke bracts. They did not throw the remaining fibrous portion away, but saved it and twisted it into twine for fish-nets. The shoots are said to be a good laxative, but should not be taken on an empty stomach. Haida women ate them to purify the blood and make themselves beautiful. As with some other plant foods, patches of Fireweed close to Haida villages were often owned by certain high-class people, and others had to ask permission to pick the stems.

The Saanich did not eat Fireweed stems but steeped the young leaves to make a tea. The Nuxalk ate the inner stems of Fireweed, as well as those of a closely related species known as River-beauty (*E. latifolium*).

Ground Cone (Broomrape Family)

Boschniakia hookeri Walpers (Orobanchaceae)

Other Name: Poque.

Botanical Description
Ground Cone is a dark purple-to-yellow parasite that grows on the roots of Salal. It is 8 to 12 cm tall and about 3 cm thick, resembling a Sitka Spruce cone standing upright on the ground. It grows alone or in clusters and each has a round, corm-like base. The small purplish flowers are crowded between the upper scales. The seed capsules are fleshy, whitish, elongated, 1 to 1.5 cm long, and rounded at the end.

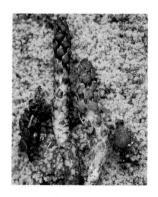

Habitat: shaded coastal forests, almost always beneath Salal plants, although it sometimes grows on Kinnikinnick and some other plants.

Distribution in British Columbia: along or near the coast, west of the coastal mountains, from Vancouver Island to northern British Columbia and the Alaska Panhandle.

Aboriginal Use

The Kwakwa̲ka'wakw, Nuu-chah-nulth and possibly some other coastal aboriginal groups, ate the potato-like stem bases of Ground Cones, usually raw as a snack, but not in any quantity. The Kwakwa̲ka'wakw name of this plant, *p'ukw'es*, apparently gave rise to the alternative English common name, Poque.

Western Dock	*Rumex occidentalis* **Wats.**
(Knotweed Family)	**(Polygonaceae)**

Other Names: Yellow Dock, "Indian Rhubarb".

Botanical Description

Western Dock is a tap-rooted, herbaceous perennial, 1 to 2 metres tall, with stout, erect stems, often reddish tinged. The basal leaves are

long-stemmed, with blades 10 to 30 cm long, generally triangular, half as wide as long and round-lobed at the base, and tapering to a blunt point at the upper end. The stem leaves are progressively smaller up the stem. Small, green flowers are crowded in long, coarse terminal clusters that turn reddish and then brown as the fruits ripen.

Habitat: moist to swampy areas and meadows from the coast to inland valleys and montane flats.

Distribution in British Columbia: fairly widespread throughout the province, but most common along the immediate coast from Vancouver Island to Alaska.

Aboriginal Use

The Saanich cooked and ate the young stems of Western Dock "just like rhubarb is today". The red-coloured stems do resemble thin stalks of rhubarb. The Nuxalk gathered the young leaves in spring, cooked them, mashed them up with Grease and ate them "like spinach". The Haida cooked and ate the leaves; since the late 1800s, they have cooked the red-coloured stems, mixed with sugar, and made jam, which was sometimes mixed with strawberry jam. The Haida call rhubarb by the same name as Western Dock, and the latter is now specifically referred to as Haida-rhubarb. Dock may have been eaten by other coastal groups, but the Kwakwaka'wakw apparently used it only as a medicine.

Sea Milkwort

Glaux maritima L. ssp. *obtusifolia* (Fernald) Boivin

(Primrose Family)

(Primulaceae)

Botanical Description
Sea Milkwort is a low, herbaceous perennial with shallow, creeping rhizomes. The leaves grow in opposing pairs spaced evenly along the stem. They are light green and slightly fleshly, smooth-edged, and somewhat elongated, 5 to 25 mm long. The flowers are minute and whitish-pink, clustered at the stem nodes. The seed capsules are small and rounded.

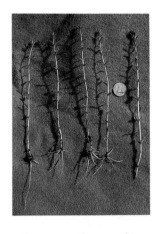

Habitat: moist, saline marshes and estuarine flats in muddy to sandy soil.

Distribution in British Columbia: restricted to coastal areas from Vancouver Island to Alaska; another subspecies occurs in the Chilcotin area and the Rocky Mountain Trench.

Aboriginal Use
The Kwakwaka'wakw, Sechelt, and Comox ate the fleshy rhizomes of Sea Milkwort, although the Nuxalk and Haida had no name or use for it, at least according to contemporary consultants. The Sechelt dug up the roots from the Porpoise Bay flats in late summer along with the roots of Pacific Cinquefoil. The Comox dug them up in fall at Bute and Toba inlets. Kwakwaka'wakw women marked the plants in the summer and returned the following spring to dig up the roots

before the plants had sprouted. They washed them and piled them in a kettle over a layer of red-hot stones. Covered, the roots were allowed to boil for a long time. The Kwakw<u>aka</u>'wakw ate Sea Milkwort rhizomes only at family meals, not at tribal feasts, dipping them in Grease and eating them with the fingers. Eating the roots made one feel sleepy, so they were usually eaten in the evening before bed. If too many were eaten, they would make one feel sick – one of the Kwakw<u>aka</u>'wakw names for the plant means "squeamish".

Saskatoon Berry (Rose Family)
Amelanchier alnifolia Nutt. (Rosaceae)

Other Names: Service Berry, June Berry, Shad-bush.

Botanical Description
Saskatoon Berry is a highly variable deciduous shrub, 1 to 7 metres tall, with smooth, reddish to grey bark and numerous round or oval leaves. The leaves are bluish-green and usually sharply toothed around the top half. The flowers, which bloom in April and May, are

white and showy, with five elongated petals, and are crowded in drooping to erect clusters. The ripe berries are dark blue and often seedy. Their size, texture and taste vary considerably depending on the individual plant or variety, the time of collection and the locality.

Habitat: dry forests and open hillsides in well-drained soil; common along rocky coastlines.

Distribution in British Columbia: common and widespread throughout the province. It is highly variable and botanists still do not agree whether it is one species or a complex of several. Coastal populations are sometimes designated as *A. florida.*

Aboriginal Use

Although Saskatoon Berries never attained the same importance to coastal First Peoples as they did for interior peoples, they were eaten by virtually every coastal group, and were highly regarded by all. The Kwakwaka'wakw and Haida names for these berries mean "sweet berry". As a Haida elder said, "That's the sweetest kind of berry you could ever get." Most groups dried them in cakes, like Salal berries. Sometimes they were mixed with other less-palatable kinds of berries.

Black Hawthorn (Rose Family)

Crataegus douglasii Lindl. (Rosaceae)

Other Names: Thornberry, Black Haw.

Botanical Description

Black Hawthorn is a large, bushy, deciduous shrub or low tree up to 10 metres tall, with greyish bark and short, stout thorns along the twig nodes. The leaves are thick, dark green and roughly egg-shaped, with the narrow end at the base and several coarse teeth around the top. The flowers are white, in showy, flattened clusters, blooming in April or May. The berries, in hanging bunches, are shiny black-purple, resembling miniature apples. They have a pleasant flavour, though sometimes bitter, but are rather dry and have large seeds.

Habitat: damp meadows, thickets and roadsides, especially along waterways and shorelines.

Distribution in British Columbia: widespread in the province south of 55° latitude, especially on southern Vancouver Island and the dry interior, but also in the Skeena River valley and on Haida Gwaii.

Aboriginal Use

The Straits Salish, Halq'emeylem, Nuu-chah-nulth, Kwakwaka'wakw, Nuxalk, Haida and Tsimshian ate the dry, seedy fruit of Black Hawthorn. The Songhees in the Victoria area ate them fresh with salmon roe. The Nuxalk considered them of poor quality, saying they caused "griping of the stomach" if too many were eaten. They believed that consuming a large quantity made one susceptible to visitations by supernatural beings. Nowadays, the Nuxalk make them into jam. The Gitksan, an Interior Tsimshian group, ate the fresh berries or boiled them for a long time in a cedar box, mashed them and stored them for winter when they were served with Grease, salmon oil or the grease of marmot, Black Bear or Grizzly Bear to relieve some of the dryness.

Tall Stawberry (*F. vesca*) flowers and fruit.

Wild Strawberries:

Seaside Strawberry   *Fragaria chiloensis* **(L.) Duchesne**
Tall Strawberry   *F. vesca* **L.**
Blue-leaf Strawberry   *F. virginiana* **Duchesne**
(Rose Family)   **(Rosaceae)**

Botanical Description
Wild strawberries are low, herbaceous perennials with conspicuous runners (stolons) for vegetative reproduction. The leaves are basal, long-stemmed, and compound, having three coarsely toothed, equal-size leaflets resembling those of cultivated strawberries, but smaller. The flowers are white and have five petals; they are often 2 cm across and there are usually several per stem. The berries, when ripe, are soft and red, resembling miniature cultivated strawberries.

Habitat: *Fragaria chiloensis* grows in rock crevices and sand near the ocean, while the other two species grow in open woodlands and clearings.

Distribution in British Columbia: *Fragaria chiloensis* is restricted to the immediate coast, and is the only species of strawberry on Haida Gwaii; *F. vesca* is common in the southern part of the province and rare in the northern half; and *F. virginiana* is found generally through-out the province, but is most common in the interior.

Aboriginal Use
The berries, juicy and delicious, were, and still are, eaten by all coastal aboriginal groups, although only the Seaside Strawberry (*F. chiloensis*) was available to the Haida. They used to pick many buckets of these along the shore, but since deer have been introduced to Haida Gwaii, the numbers of strawberries have been drastically reduced. Nuxalk children used to search the woods for strawberries in the month of July, crying out, "*kwululuu-tsuu-tsu!*" ("I've found another strawberry!"), whenever they came across a patch of them or even a single one.

    Strawberries were usually eaten fresh, being too juicy to dry like other types of berries. The Saanich and Comox steeped the fresh leaves in boiling water to make a clear, sweet tea; the Comox often mixed them with the leaves of Thimbleberry and Trailing Wild Blackberry.

Indian Plum   *Oemlaria cerasiformis* (T. & G.) Landon
(Rose Family)   (Rosaceae)

Other Names: Bird-cherry, Oso-berry, Skunk Bush.

Botanical Description

Indian Plum is a tall, deciduous shrub, up to 5 metres tall, having a peculiar pungent odour. In spring, it produces leaves and flowers earlier than any other shrub. The bark is smooth and grey, or reddish on

young twigs. The leaves are bright green, oblong, tapered at both ends but widest above the middle, and smooth-edged. The small white flowers, growing in drooping clusters, appear before the leaves have fully grown. Male and female flowers grow on separate bushes but look similar. The fruits resemble small clustered plums, at first yellowish-red, ripening to dark blue. They have large stones and can be bitter and "choky", especially when unripe. *Oemleria cerasiformis* is also known as *Osmaronia cerasiformis* and *Nuttallia cerasiformis*.

Habitat: moist, open woods and roadside thickets.

Distribution in British Columbia: restricted to the extreme southwest corner of the province; common around Victoria and Vancouver.

Aboriginal Use

The Straits Salish, Halq'emeylem, Squamish and several Washington Salish groups ate the fruits fresh or sometimes dried, but not in large quantities. Some aboriginal people call them "choke-cherries" because they are bitter and make you pucker, but they are quite palatable when fully ripe.

The Kwakwaka'wakw ate a type of fruit they described as Indian Plum, which they obtained from a restricted area at the upper reaches of Knight Inlet, although *Oemleria* has not been recorded from there.

They ate these fresh with plenty of Grease at family meals and feasts. Inexperienced eaters had to use large quantities of oil because the fruit was dry and hard to swallow. However, one was never allowed to drink water with them. To store them for winter, the Kwakwaka'wakw put them in tall cedar boxes, covered them with hot oil, sealed the boxes and put them in a cool place.

Pacific Cinquefoil (Rose Family)

Potentilla pacifica Howell (Rosaceae)

Other Name: Pacific Silverweed.

Botanical Description

Pacific Cinquefoil is a low, herbaceous perennial with spreading runners and long, thick roots. The leaves, basal and clumped, are 20 to 40 cm long and are pinnately compound, with usually 13 to 15 oval, sharply toothed leaflets, decreasing in size towards the base of the leaf. They are green on the upper surface and silvery-white beneath, suggesting the name, Silverweed. The yellow flowers resemble buttercups at first glance. They grow singly on long stalks. *Potentilla pacifica* is sometimes called *P. anserina* ssp. *pacifica*.

Habitat: coastal dunes, beaches, salt marshes and estuarine flats, frequently growing in extensive patches.

Distribution in British Columbia: along the entire coast, from Vancouver Island to Alaska. A closely related species, *P. anserina*, is found east of the Coast Mountains in saline marshes and around alkali lakes.

Aboriginal Use

Almost all coastal aboriginal groups harvested the long, brown-skinned roots of Pacific Cinquefoil. They frequently associated them with Springbank Clover rhizomes, since Cinquefoil grows in the same habitat and people collected and prepared them in the same way; but Clover roots are thinner and white-skinned. As with Clover, Cinquefoil patches were often "owned" by certain chiefs, especially among the Nuu-chah-nulth, Kwakwaka'wakw and Haida. Others were not allowed to dig them without asking permission, and sometimes had to pay for the privilege. Like Clover, Cinquefoil has two types of roots: short, curly roots near the surface, and long, fleshy taproots. Women dug them up in late fall or early spring. They never ate Cinquefoil roots raw, because they are bitter. Steam-cooked, they taste like sweet potatoes, though they can still be bitter.

To the Nuu-chah-nulth, they were second only to Bracken Fern rhizomes in importance as a root vegetable. The Sechelt dug them up, along with Sea Milkwort rhizomes, in the mud flats at Porpoise Bay. The Nuxalk obtained them locally, from the tidal flats at the mouth of the Bella Coola River, and often mixed them with Clover roots for cooking.

The Kwakwaka'wakw preferred Cinquefoil roots from Knight and Kingcome inlets; those from the Nimpkish River flats were said to be too gnarled from the gravelly soil. They put the short roots in baskets and coiled up the long ones, tying them in bundles. They dried them or stored them fresh in a cool place. According to Kwakwaka'wakw tradition, the men cooked Cinquefoil roots at a feast. They packed alternating layers of curly and long roots over red-hot rocks and dried fern leaves in a tall, cedar steaming box, poured hot water over them and covered them with a mat; they left them to cook until the mat sank down, indicating that the roots had softened. Then they removed the roots, separated them and allowed them to cool. They served the roots on dishes, each accommodating six people. The chiefs and high-class people ate the long roots, rolling them into a ball to place in the mouth; the commoners ate the curly roots. Guests were permitted to drink water after a Cinquefoil feast, and they could take leftovers home to their wives. For a family meal, the roots were boiled in a kettle instead of a box. Later, they added sugar to them to counteract some of the bitterness.

Wild Crabapple
(Rose Family)

Malus fusca Raf.
(Rosaceae)

Other Names: Pacific Crabapple, Oregon Crabapple, Western Crabapple.

Botanical Description

Wild Crabapple is a small, scraggly tree, sometimes shrub-like, 3 to 8 metres tall, with rough, grey bark on the trunk. The leaves, deep green and 4 to 10 cm long, are similar in shape to orchard apple leaves, but often have a prominent pointed lobe along one or both edges. The flowers are white to pinkish and smaller than orchard apple blossoms; they grow in flattened clusters of five to twelve. The fruits hang in long-stemmed clusters. They are small, elongated, yellow to purplish-red when ripe, and very tart; after a frost, they turn brown and soft. Synonyms for *Malus fusca* are *Pyrus fusca* and *P. diversifolia.*

Habitat: moist woods, swamps and bogs, and along waterways, often in dense thickets.

Distribution in British Columbia: west of the coastal mountains from Vancouver Island to Alaska, up to 800 metres elevation.

Aboriginal Use

Wild Crabapples were an important food for all coastal aboriginal groups in the province. They were generally harvested in late summer, when full-size but still green, and allowed to ripen during storage. Some groups, such as the Sechelt, picked them after the first frost when they were soft and brown. Crabapples were usually picked and stored in bunches with the stems still attached.

The Straits Salish, Halq'emeylem, Squamish and Nuu-chah-nulth often hung Crabapples in cat-tail bags until they were ripe, then ate them raw or cooked, sometimes mashing them and mixing them with other fruit such as Salal. They boiled the hard, acidic Crabapples until they softened; the Nuu-chah-nulth – and perhaps some other groups – steamed the mushy ones in pits. In Nuu-chah-nulth territory, Crabapples were said to be most plentiful and of greatest importance at the head of the Alberni Canal, although they grew sporadically along the west coast of Vancouver Island. According to Sproat (1868), the Nuu-chah-nulth people were as careful of their Crabapple trees as Europeans were of their orchards. When European settlers began to encroach on aboriginal land, the Nuu-chah-nulth were bitterly resentful and cut down all the Wild Crabapple trees around the colonial settlements so that their last crop of fruit would at least be easy to harvest.

Central and northern aboriginal groups, including the Kwakwaka'wakw, Nuxalk, Haisla, Tsimshian and Haida, stored Crabapples as they did High-bush Cranberries. They kept them, either raw or boiled until soft, in water in tall cedar boxes until the time of the winter ceremonials when they ate them at large feasts. The Kwakwaka'wakw removed the stems beforehand, while the Haida destemmed and sorted the fruit just before a feast. They drained the juice from the Crabapples (and saved it for some later time), mixed them with Grease and ate them with spoons, swallowing only the juicy part and spitting out the skins and seeds. The Kwakwaka'wakw and Haida often mashed them with Salal berries and, in recent times, added sugar. Kwakwaka'wakw families sometimes ate raw Crabapples alone, without oil, biting them off, one at a time, from intact clusters.

Crabapples were a common item of trade and commerce, especially among the northern groups. At the turn of the century a single box of Crabapples in water might cost about ten pairs of Hudson's Bay blankets (worth $10 altogether). A wedding gift between high-class families might include, among other things, ten boxes of Crabapples and five boxes of Grease to put on them. Crabapples are the most frequently mentioned fruit in Tsimshian stories. They are still eaten today in many areas, either cooked and mashed in the traditional way, or made into jelly. They are usually stored by freezing.

Wild Roses:

Common Wild Rose	*Rosa nutkana* **K. Presl**
Swamp Rose	*R. pisocarpa* **A. Gray**
Dwarf Wild Rose	*R. gymnocarpa* **Nutt.**
(Rose Family)	**(Rosaceae)**

Other Names: Nootka Rose (*R. nutkana*).

Botanical Description

Common Wild Rose.

All wild roses are erect shrubs, with spiny or thorny stems and compound leaves with usually five to seven toothed leaflets, similar to garden rose leaves but smaller. They have pale to bright pink, five-petalled flowers with yellow centres, and red-orange fruits or hips composed of a fleshy outer rind and many whitish seeds in the centre. The rind is bland-tasting but high in Vitamin C. Common Wild Rose (*R. nutkana*) has large, curved spines, reddish stems and large, single flowers. Swamp Rose (*R. pisocarpa*) has smaller, straight spines and smaller flowers, usually in clusters of three to six. Dwarf Wild Rose (*R. gymnocarpa*) has numerous small spines crowded along the stem; the flowers and fruits usually grow singly and are much smaller than those of the other two species.

Habitat: Common Wild Rose is common along roadsides and shore-lines, and in meadows and open woods, often forming dense thickets; Swamp Rose grows in open, swampy meadows, also forming thickets; and Dwarf Wild Rose is usually found in shaded coastal woods.

Distribution in British Columbia: Common Wild Rose is wide-spread in the province; Swamp Rose grows only in the southwestern corner, on Vancouver Island, the Gulf Islands and the Lower Mainland; and Dwarf Wild Rose is restricted to the southern part of the province, south of about 52° latitude.

Fruits, or hips, of the Common Wild Rose (left) and Dwarf Wild Rose (right).

Aboriginal Use

The use of wild rose hips as food by coastal First Peoples varies considerably from group to group. Most western Washington Salish groups ate the fruit of Common Wild Rose; apparently, only the Squaxin ate Swamp Rose fruit; and none used the hips of Dwarf Wild Rose. The Vancouver Island Salish seem to have used all three types, picking them in autumn and eating the red-orange outer rind raw. They also peeled and ate the tender young shoots of Common Wild Rose in spring.

The Sto:lo, Squamish, Sechelt, Nuu-chah-nulth and Kwakwa̲ka̲'-wakw did not traditionally eat any variety. One Kwakwa̲ka̲'wakw woman, when asked if her people had eaten rose hips, laughed and said, "Oh no! They would give you an itchy bottom!" The Comox also attributed this effect to the seeds, but ate the outer rind. The Nuxalk ate the fruit rinds of both Common and Dwarf wild roses in late fall, and the Haida and Tsimshian ate those of Common Wild Rose, the only species extending that far north. Haida women peeled and ate the young shoots as a tonic and beauty aid, but apparently not as a regular food.

Cloudberry
(Rose Family)

Rubus chamaemorus L.
(Rosaceae)

Other Names: Baked-apple, Malt-berry, Mars Apple, Foxberry.

Botanical Description

Cloudberry is a low, herbaceous perennial with long, creeping rhizomes. The stems are unbranched, slender and wiry, up to 30 cm tall (but usually shorter), with one to three leaves. The leaves are dark green and broader than they are long; they usually have five lobes, rounded and sharply toothed on the margins. The white flowers are solitary and terminal, with male and female flowers on separate plants. Many plants are sterile, lacking flowers or fruits. The berries are compound, like a raspberry, but the drupelets are fewer and larger. Unripe berries are hard and reddish; they turn soft and salmon-coloured as they ripen. Their sour-bitter taste is unpleasant when first encountered, but more agreeable with experience.

Habitat: muskegs and peat bogs, in association with Sphagnum moss.

Distribution in British Columbia: sporadic in peat bogs on Vancouver Island and the Lower Mainland, but usually not fruiting; common in the muskegs of Graham Island on Haida Gwaii, and widespread in the northern half of the province in appropriate habitats.

Aboriginal Use

The Haida and Tsimshian once ate Cloudberries in large quantities. They picked the still-hard berries in mid summer and stored them in water in tall boxes, or more recently, in barrels or in the freezer. The Massett Haida gathered them locally, but also imported them from the Skeena River area. At one time, canned Mars Apples were sold in the Masset Co-op Store for $1.25 a pound, but these were canned improperly, without cooking, in the days when canning techniques were not well understood in this area, and most of them spoiled.

Cloudberries make excellent jam, and were extremely popular on Haida Gwaii, but fruiting plants have become rare since deer were introduced to the islands. Nowadays, the sight of Cloudberries inspires mouth-watering memories in old Haida people; many younger people have never tasted them.

Wild Raspberry
(Rose Family)

Rubus idaeus L.
(Rosaceae)

Botanical Description

Wild Raspberry is a prickly shrub similar to cultivated raspberries but usually shorter and not as robust. The bark is brownish and the leaves are mostly compound, with three (or five) sharply pointed leaflets, of which the terminal one is largest, like garden raspberry leaves. The flowers are white and inconspicuous, growing in small clusters. The berries are bright red, or occasionally yellow, like garden raspberries but smaller and of better flavour.

Habitat: stream banks, talus slopes, open woods and clearings.

Distribution in British Columbia: widespread in the interior and reaching the coast along some of the northern river valleys such as the Bella Coola and Skeena; not on Vancouver Island or Haida Gwaii.

Aboriginal Use

The Nuxalk and Tsimshian, and possibly the Haisla and northern Kwakwaka'wakw, ate Wild Raspberries – these were the only groups that had access to them. They ate them fresh, or boiled and dried in cakes for winter. In the 1970s, the Nuxalk were still gathering them in large quantities from the logged-off hillsides in Tweedsmuir Park, along with wild gooseberries, Blackcaps and other types of berries. Nowadays, Wild Raspberries are frozen or made into jam. They are sweet and delicious, one of the most popular types of fruit in this area.

Blackcap
(Rose Family)

Rubus leucodermis Dougl.
(Rosaceae)

Other Name: Black Raspberry.

Botanical Description

Blackcap is a raspberry-like shrub with long, arching branches and numerous recurved prickles along the stems. The bark is smooth and greenish to red, but has a thick, waxy coating that gives it a characteristic blue-grey cast. The leaves, prickly veined and white beneath, are compound like raspberry leaves, consisting of two lateral leaflets and a larger terminal one, all sharply toothed. The flowers are white, often clustered, and the berries are dark purplish-black, similar to raspberries but shorter and finer. When ripe, they fall off readily. Some people regard them as sweet and juicy, but others find them bland and too seedy.

Habitat: open woods, burns and clearings.

Distribution in British Columbia: throughout the southern part of the province, as far north as the Bella Coola River valley, but generally south of 51° latitude.

Aboriginal Use

The Straits Salish, Sto:lo, Squamish, Sechelt, Comox, Kwakwaka'-wakw and Nuxalk ate Blackcap berries fresh, or dried in cakes. The Upper Sto:lo dried them like raisins on mats in the sun. They are still eaten today, especially by the Nuxalk, who make them into jam along with Wild Raspberries. The Comox also eat the young shoots, peeled, in spring.

Thimbleberry
(Rose Family)

Rubus parviflorus Nutt.
(Rosaceae)

Botanical Description
Thimbleberry is an erect, many-stemmed shrub, usually 1 to 1.5 metres tall on the coast (but taller inland). The bark is light brown, thin and shredded. The leaves are large and light green, with five pointed lobes, like maple leaves; they are marginally toothed and finely fuzzy on both sides. The flowers are large and white, growing in few-to-many-flowered terminal clusters. The berries turn from green to white to pink to bright red as they ripen. They are shallowly cup-shaped and, when ripe, fall easily from their stems. Their taste varies with weather and locality, but ideally, they are sweet and flavourful, though somewhat seedy.

Habitat: in open woods and clearings, and along roadsides and shorelines, often forming dense thickets.

Distribution in British Columbia: widespread in the lower two-thirds of the province, south of 55° latitude; common on the coast north to Haida Gwaii.

Aboriginal Use
All coastal aboriginal groups in the province harvested and ate Thimbleberries, and also the young Thimbleberry sprouts as a green vegetable. They gathered the sprouts in early spring through early summer, and ate them raw and peeled; the sprouts are sweet and juicy. Sproat (1868), in his writings on Nuu-chah-nulth, remarked that during the summer, "canoes may be seen laden with these shoots".

The berries, having a coarse, seedy texture, lend themselves to drying. Philip Drucker (1951) states that they were the only type of berry dried by the Nuu-chah-nulth, other than Salal. The Nuu-chah-nulth made a special type of berry cake, laying out sticks of roasted clams in parallel fashion on a board, covering them with a layer of fresh Thimbleberries, then another layer of strung clams, and so on. Then they laid a length of plank on top of the pile and pressed the clams and Thimbleberries together into a compact loaf, using stones, or sometimes a woman sat on the plank. They sun-dried the flattened cake, then stored it for later use.

The Kwakwa̱ka'wakw picked Thimbleberries when they were still hard and pink, leaving the stems attached. They put them into a cedar-bark bag or (later) a pillowcase, sprinkled a little water over them, and left them for a day or so until the berries turned red. Then they destemmed the ripe berries and ate them fresh, or dried them in the usual fashion. The Nuxalk often cooked Thimbleberries with other types of berries such as Wild Raspberries, before drying them. They considered Thimbleberries to be inferior to Wild Raspberries and Blackcaps.

Trailing Wild Raspberry (Rose Family)

Rubus pedatus J.E. Smith (Rosaceae)

Botanical Description

Trailing Wild Raspberry is a low, trailing herbaceous perennial with stems up to 1 metre long, frequently rooting. The leaves are compound with three to five sharply toothed leaflets extending radially from the stem. The flowers, borne on short stems, are white and inconspicuous. The berries are red and look like raspberries, but with only two to five drupelets each. They are not particularly flavourful.

Habitat: from mossy banks to moist woods, from sea-level to the timberline.

Distribution in British Columbia: widespread throughout the province, but in the south restricted to montane forests.

Aboriginal Use

The Haida called these "Steller's Jay berries" (Massett dialect) or "ground-berries" (Skidegate dialect). The Haida ate Trailing Wild Raspberries, even though they are small, soft and difficult to pick in any quantity, often mixing them with Bog Cranberries. They had to cook them a long time. Apparently, other aboriginal groups on the coast did not bother with these berries because they are so small.

Salmonberry	*Rubus spectabilis* Pursh
(Rose Family)	**(Rosaceae)**

Botanical Description

Salmonberry is a tall, raspberry-like shrub with reddish-brown bark and numerous short prickles along the stems. The leaves, like those of

Salmonberry flowers and gold-type berries (below).

raspberries, are compound, with two lateral leaflets and one larger terminal one. The flowers, usually solitary, bloom early in the spring before the leaves have fully expanded. They are pink and fairly showy. The berries resemble large, deeply cupped raspberries and come in a range of colours, from salmon or gold to deep ruby red to almost black. Berries of different colour grow on different bushes, but all can be found in the same locality. They are juicy, but can be insipid and quite seedy.

Habitat: shaded swamps, damp woods and moist clearings along roads and shorelines, often forming large thickets.

Distribution in British Columbia: abundant along the coast from Vancouver Island to Alaska, but mainly west of the Coast Mountains.

Aboriginal Use

All coastal aboriginal groups in the province ate both sprouts and berries in large quantities. The sprouts, like those of Thimbleberry, were picked in spring, peeled and eaten raw or occasionally steamed. The central and northern groups usually dipped them in Grease or dried salmon spawn. All groups often ate the sprouts with salmon. Salmonberries are one of the earliest ripening berries, usually in May and June. Coastal First Peoples picked both the gold and ruby forms, and usually ate them fresh because they are too watery to dry in cakes like other berries. Families or individuals in some groups

"owned" Salmonberry patches, as they did other types of plant foods. A Nuu-chah-nulth owner claimed the right to the first and second picking of his berries, sending a party of women from his house to harvest them. After many boxes had been collected, the chief used them to give a feast. Following this event anyone could pick from his bushes.

Both Salmonberries and Salmonberry sprouts are still eaten today, usually with sugar. They are especially favoured by children.

Salmonberry and Thimbleberry sprouts, peeled and ready to eat.

Trailing Wild Blackberry

(Rose Family)

Rubus ursinus Cham. & Schlecht.
(Rosaceae)

Other Name: Pacific Blackberry.

Botanical Description
Trailing Wild Blackberry is a low, trailing, woody perennial with prickly stems up to several metres long. The bark is smooth and covered with a waxy coating, giving it a blue-grey appearance. The leaves resemble garden blackberry or raspberry leaves, being compound with

two lateral leaflets and one larger terminal leaflet on a short stem. The leaf margins are sharply toothed and the stems and veins are prickly. Male and female flowers grow on separate plants but look similar, being white with elongated petals; they usually grow in small clusters. The fruits are of the same general shape and character as loganberries or boysenberries but smaller and shiny black when ripe. They are sweet and juicy.

Habitat: open to dense woods and exposed clearings, especially in burned and logged-over areas.

Distribution in British Columbia: restricted to the southwestern corner of the province, southern Vancouver Island and the adjacent mainland, but often very common within this range.

Aboriginal Use
The Straits Salish, Halq'emeylem, Squamish, Sechelt, Comox, Nuu-chah-nulth and Kwakwaka'wakw ate Trailing Wild Blackberries fresh, or mashed and dried in cakes. Even some Haida people recall eating them when at school on the Lower Mainland; they called the plant "Ground Salmonberry", recognizing it as a close relative of the species so common on Haida Gwaii. The Saanich, Sechelt and Comox boiled the old red leaves of Trailing Wild Blackberry to make a refreshing tea. Though the plant is deciduous, the old leaves often remain on the stems over the winter, so this tea is available all year round.

Sitka Mountain Ash
(Rose Family)

Sorbus sitchensis Roemer
(Rosaceae)

Botanical Description

Sitka Mountain Ash is a low tree or bushy shrub, up to 4 metres tall, closely related to the mountain ash or rowan tree grown in city gardens and often found naturalized around Victoria and Vancouver. Like its relative, the Sitka Mountain Ash has grey bark and pinnately compound leaves. The leaflets number seven to eleven, are elongated, rounded and sharply toothed around the top half. The flowers

are small and white, crowded in flat-topped clusters. The berries are red-orange and soft, with yellowish flesh. They are extremely tart and bitter. *Sorbus sitchensis* is also known as *S. occidentalis.*

Habitat: open woods and clearings, usually subalpine in the southern part of its range but at lower elevations northwards.

Distribution in British Columbia: common throughout the province except in the far northeast.

Aboriginal Use

Coastal First Peoples did not generally eat the berries of Sitka Mountain Ash. The Haida sometimes ate them, but did not regard them highly. The Nuxalk rubbed them on the scalp to combat lice and dandruff. Now, the berries are sometimes used to make jelly.

Black Cottonwood

(Willow Family)

Populus trichocarpa T. & G. ex Hook.
(Salicaceae)

Botanical Description

Black Cottonwood is a rough-barked, deciduous tree, up to 50 metres tall. The spring buds and leaves are resinous and sweet-smelling. The leaves are long-stemmed and generally heart-shaped or triangular, rounded at the bottom and sharply pointed at the tip, with finely toothed margins. In early spring they are characteristically yellow-green.

 Male and female flowers are on separate trees. They are long, pendulant catkins; at fruiting time, the female catkins are covered with soft downy "cotton" which is released along with the seeds in mid summer, filling the air with bits of white fluff resembling snowflakes.

Habitat: alluvial flood plains, stream banks, lake shores and swamps; able to withstand periodic flooding.

Distribution in British Columbia: common at low and middle elevations throughout the province, except for the far northeastern corner and Haida Gwaii.

Aboriginal Use

The Nuxalk and Northern Kwakwaka'wakw ate cottonwood cambium in May and early June. They pulled off the bark of moderately sized trees and scraped off the cambium and secondary phloem tissues with a knife. They ate it fresh or sun-dried with Grease. Black Cottonwood cambium is extremely sweet, but it sours or ferments rapidly, so it cannot be stored for winter use like that of Western Hemlock.

Stinging Nettle
(Nettle Family)

Urtica dioica L.
(Urticaceae)

Other Names: Indian Spinach, Northwest Nettle.

Botanical Description

A herbaceous perennial, Stinging Nettle grows 1 to 3 metres tall, with spreading rhizomes. The ragged-looking leaves grow in opposite pairs along the stem. They are 7 to 15 cm long on short stems, rounded at the base, broadest below the middle and tapering to a sharp point. The edges are sharply toothed. The greenish, inconspicuous flowers are clustered in drooping bunches at the stem nodes. The leaves and stems are covered with stiff hairs that cause stinging and blistering when touched. Another name for *Urtica dioica* is *U. lyallii.*

Habitat: edges of clearings and old fields, and in damp roadside thickets and shaded woods, usually growing in large patches.

Distribution in British Columbia: common along the coast from Vancouver Island to Alaska, and in the southern and central interior.

Aboriginal Use

The young leaves and stems of the Stinging Nettle were cooked and eaten by the Saanich, Cowichan, Kwakwa̲ka'wakw, Sechelt and Haida, but apparently not by the Comox, Nuu-chah-nulth, Nuxalk and Tsimshian. The Haida also ate the rhizomes, but apparently more as a medicine than a food. Generally, harvesters of Stinging Nettles gathered the young shoots just as they were appearing from the ground, then boiled and ate them as we eat spinach. The stinging properties disappear with cooking, but care must be taken when harvesting the plants. The Gitksan, an interior Tsimshian group, made a tea from the leaves but only as a medicine.

APPENDIX 1

Some Non-native Food Plants Used by Coastal First Peoples

Onions (*Allium cepa* L.)
Lily Family (Liliaceae)
Onions have been imported and cultivated by a number of coastal aboriginal groups since the early 1900s. Groups familiar with wild onions called the cultivated type by the same name. The Haida, having no wild onions on Haida Gwaii, call them *anyes*, after the English name.

Rice (*Oryza sativa* L.)
Grass Family (Poaceae or Gramineae)
Acquired from Europeans through trade fairly early in the history of contact, rice was usually associated with the bulbs of Mission Bells (*Fritillaria camschatcensis*), which later came to be called Rice Root or Indian Rice. In Haida, rice was called "Fritillaria teeth", the same name given to the small bulblets around the main bulb of Rice Root.

Carrots (*Daucus carota* L.)
Celery Family (Apiaceae or Umbelliferae)
Carrots were commonly cultivated by coastal First Peoples since the early 1900s. Groups such as Straits Salish and Kwakwaka'wakw, having a "Wild Carrot" counterpart (see Pacific Hemlock-parsley and Wild Caraway), called the introduced carrot by the same name.

Parsnips (*Pastinaca sativa* L.)
Celery Family (Apiaceae or Umbelliferae)
Parsnips were also commonly cultivated by coastal First Peoples since the early 1900s, especially by the Nuxalk, who called them by the same name as an unidentified type of wild parsnip.

Turnips (*Brassica rapa* L. group)
Mustard Family (Brassicaceae or Cruciferae)
After potatoes, turnips were probably the most commonly cultivated vegetable, at least among the northern coastal groups. Like potatoes, they were introduced to the coast fairly early in the history of contact with Europeans and soon became a staple crop, especially among the Haida. The Haida and Nuxalk names for turnips are the same – *yanahu* – indicating some kind of knowledge transfer between the two groups.

Watercress (*Rorippa nasturtium-aquaticum* (L.) Schinz & Thell.)
Mustard Family (Brassicaceae or Cruciferae)
Watercress is a weedy plant of stream banks, introduced from Europe. The Saanich used to pick it at Shady Creek near Brentwood on Vancouver Island and eat the leaves raw, a practice probably learned from the local colonists.

Beans (*Phaseolus vulgaris* L.)
Pea Family (Fabaceae or Leguminosae)
Beans were imported and cultivated by coastal First Peoples since the late 1800s. In the Haida language, they were named "Raven's canoe", after the seed pods of the Giant Vetch and some other wild legumes.

Peas (*Pisum sativum* L.)
Pea Family (Fabaceae or Leguminosae)
The Haida also called peas "Raven's canoe", as they did garden beans, after the pods of the Giant Vetch.

Currants and gooseberries (*Ribes* spp.)
Gooseberry Family (Grossulariaceae)
Several varieties of cultivated currants and gooseberries were – and still are – grown in the gardens of coastal First Peoples. They are generally named after their wild counterparts. In Nuxalk, red garden currants are named after Red Huckleberries.

Rhubarb (*Rheum hybridum* Murr.)
Knotweed Family (Polygonaceae)
Rhubarb is commonly cultivated, even today, by coastal First Peoples. It is generally associated with Western Dock or Cow Parsnip. Rhubarb is often made into jam, sometimes mixed with fruit such as strawberries.

Sour-grass or Sheep Sorrel (*Rumex acetosella* L.)
Knotweed Family (Polygonaceae)
A low weed of gardens and waste places, Sour-grass was originally introduced from Europe. The Nuxalk, Saanich, Washington Chehalis and probably other aboriginal groups have learned to eat the tangy, sour leaves raw or cooked as a snack or flavouring, just as many white people do, especially children. Some Nuxalk people call it "sour plant", an improvised but appropriate name.

Tree fruits: peaches, cherries and plums (*Prunus* spp.);
apples (*Malus* spp.); and pears (*Pyrus* spp.)
Rose Family (Rosaceae)
All of these fruits, especially apples, were adopted and cultivated by coastal First Peoples. Apple orchards may still be found near some abandoned aboriginal villages along the coast. Peaches were seldom grown, but imported dried or canned and used to make wine, especially in the Bella Coola area.

Berries: raspberries and blackberries (*Rubus* spp.);
strawberries (*Fragaria* spp.)
Rose Family (Rosaceae)
These were and still are commonly cultivated by coastal First Peoples. They are usually named after their wild counterparts in the native languages. In Haida, for example, raspberries are called "white man's Salmonberries".

Oranges (*Citrus sinensis* (L.) Osb.)
Citrus Family (Rutaceae)
Coastal First Peoples began importing oranges in the twentieth century. The Haida name for orange is "stink-peel", while the Nuxalk just call them *antsns*, after the English name.

Potatoes (*Solanum tuberosum* L.)
Potato Family (Solanaceae)
Potato is without doubt the most important single crop plant for coastal First Peoples. It was introduced to the coast by some of the earliest European seamen. It was sometimes planted by them as a future food source, or was given to the aboriginal people with instructions on how to plant and harvest it. By the mid 1800s, it had become a staple food and a valuable trading item for almost all coastal aboriginal groups.

The Haida were especially proficient at growing potatoes and sold them not only to the Tsimshian on the mainland but to passing fur-trading ships and to the Hudson's Bay Company. Some of the oldest Haida people today recall seeing Haida canoes, laden almost to the gunwales with potatoes, heading across the treacherous waters of Hecate Strait en route to the Nass and Skeena rivers to trade with the Tsimshian for Grease, smoked Eulachons and other mainland products. The Haida even sold potatoes among themselves. In 1902, Dr C.F. Newcombe referred to them in his notes to a mortuary pole for a man at Cumshewa Village. The pole was raised by his wife, "who . . . was very rich, having much money in raising and selling potatoes to the villages in the neighbourhood".

An ancestor of the Young family in Skidegate, John Skedans, was one of the first Haidas to plant potatoes. He planted them at the mouth of the Copper River on Moresby Island after a big ceremony; he made a speech about potatoes, saying they would be harvested "when the Dog Salmon come up the river and their heads turn white".

Some coastal aboriginal names for potato are *sgusiit* (Massett Haida and Tsimshian), *sgawsiit* (Skidegate Haida), *kwusi* (Nuxalk) and *sqawts* (Pemberton Lillooet, an interior Salish language). These names have an obvious common origin. A number of aboriginal people believe the name was derived from the English words "good seed", which were repeated over and over by the Europeans on introducing the potato in an effort to show the natives that it was to be planted.

Few Haida people grow potatoes today, but at Bella Coola, it is not uncommon to see small clearings in the woods planted with them. As a major source of starch in an area where carbohydrates were extremely rare, their impact on the coastal aboriginal diet was immense.

Tobacco (*Nicotiana* spp.)
Potato Family (Solanaceae)

Tobacco is definitely not a food plant, but it is included here since it was used orally. The Haida and the Tlingit of Alaska formerly cultivated a type of tobacco, tentatively identified as a variety of *N. quadrivalvis*, as described by N.J. Turner and R.L. Taylor in "A Review of the Northwest Coast Tobacco Mystery" (1972). This tobacco was not smoked, but chewed with burnt clam shells. When commercial tobacco (*N. tabacum*) was introduced to the coast by European traders, it soon replaced this native tobacco, and was both chewed and smoked by virtually all coastal aboriginal groups. The practice of mixing dried Kinnikinnick leaves with it as a flavouring and to make it last longer was soon learned even in groups previously unfamiliar with Kinnikinnick as a smoking substance.

APPENDIX 2

Some Plants Considered to be Poisonous or Inedible by Coastal First Peoples*

Queenscup (*Clintonia uniflora* (Schult.) Kunth.)
Lily Family (Liliaceae)

Queenscup is a low herbaceous plant that grows in shaded montane forests in the southern two-thirds of the province. The leaves, usually

two per plant, are basal and *Erythronium*-like, tapering at each end. The flower is white and solitary on a slender stem, producing a single bright blue berry. The plant was not widely recognized by coastal First Peoples, but the Nuxalk called it "wolf's berry", believing it edible only by wolves.

Twisted Stalk (*Streptopus amplexifolius* (L.) DC.)
Lily Family (Liliaceae)

Twisted Stalk is a slender herbaceous perennial of shaded forests and

stream banks throughout the province. The stems are up to 1 metre tall, usually branching below the middle. The elliptical, pointed, clasping leaves are spaced alternately along the stem, which bends slightly at each node. Small greenish-white flowers grow singly beneath each leaf along the upper part of the stem. The fruits are elongated, reddish-orange berries, which are juicy and slightly translucent. The Haida called them "owl

---

* See also Turner and Szczawinski (1991), listed in Additional References.

berries" or "witch berries" in Skidegate, and "Black Bear berries" in Massett, and the Kwakw<u>a</u>ka'wakw called them "frog berries", the same name they gave to the edible fruits of Wild Lily-of-the-valley. All groups believed them to be inedible by humans.

Indian Hellebore (*Veratrum viride* Ait.)
Lily Family (Liliaceae)

Indian Hellebore is a tall, robust, distinctive plant of montane meadows or, occasionally, lowland swamps. It is also known as Green Hellebore or False Hellebore. The leaves, bright green and largest near the base of the plant, are broadly ellipse-shaped, pointed and conspicuously accordion-pleated longitudinally. The flowers are small and green, crowded in elongated terminal clusters. Indian Hellebore is one of the most violently poisonous plants in the province, a  fact recognized by all coastal aboriginal groups. The plant was, and still is, highly respected. It was taken with extreme caution as a medicine for innumerable ailments. But eating even a small portion of the plant can result in loss of consciousness, followed by death.

Death Camas (*Zigadenus venenosus* S. Wats.)
Lily Family (Liliaceae)

A grass-like bulb plant, Death Camas grows on the dry hillsides of southern Vancouver Island and the Gulf Islands, and also in the dry southern interior. On the coast, its range coincides with that of the Blue Camas (see page 42). Death Camas is also called White Camas or Poison Onion. The bulbs and leaves resemble those of Blue Camas, but give a burning sensation when touched to the

Death Camas growing with Blue Camas.

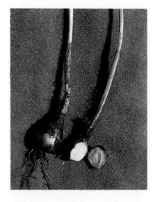

Death Camas bulbs.

tongue. The flowers are small and cream-coloured, and grow in a tight, pointed cluster. The aboriginal people within the range of this plant were well aware of its poisonous qualities, which are caused by a number of toxic alkaloids, some of them closely related to those found in Indian Hellebore. When digging Blue Camas and other edible bulbs, great care was taken not to confuse them with Death Camas bulbs. Within its area of distribution, Death Camas is responsible for the greatest loss of life to sheep of any poisonous plant.

Water Hemlock (*Cicuta douglasii* (DC.) Coult. & Rose, and related spp.)
Celery Family (Apiaceae or Umbelliferae)

The genus *Cicuta* has been described as the most poisonous in North America. Water Hemlock is a stout herbaceous perennial, 50 to 200 cm tall, with a round, thickened, chambered base, like a small turnip. The leaves are three times compound, with many small, narrow leaflets that are pointed and sharply toothed. An important feature of identification is that the leaf veins are directed to the bases of the teeth, rather than to the points. The flowers are small, white and

numerous, in flat-topped umbrella-like clusters, like those of the Cow Parsnip but smaller and more slender. The plant grows throughout the province, except on Haida Gwaii, in marshes, ditches and wet low places.

Like Indian Hellebore, Water Hemlock is recognized by coastal First Peoples as being an extremely dangerous plant (the rootstocks of one plant are enough to kill a cow), but it was taken with great caution as a medicine. Its close relationship to various edible plants, such as Cow Parsnip, Water Parsnip and Garden

Parsnip, was realized. More than one record exists of Water Hemlock having been mistaken for some edible plant, resulting in the death of one or more people.

Devil's Club (*Oplopanax horridus* (J.E. Smith) Miq.)
Ginseng Family (Araliaceae)

Devil's Club is a low, sprawling shrub, covered with numerous needle-like spines. The leaves are large and maple-like, also spiny along the veins. The flowers are small and whitish, in a pyramidal terminal cluster. The berries, when ripe, are bright red, flattened and slightly spiny. Devil's Club is common in damp montane forests along the coast, and east to the Selkirk Mountains. Some people are highly allergic to the spines. The berries were considered inedible by all coastal aboriginal groups. The Haida rubbed them on the scalp to combat lice and dandruff and to make the hair shiny. The Nuxalk called them "Grizzly Bear berries", believing them to be the Grizzly's High-bush Cranberries.

Orange Honeysuckle (*Lonicera ciliosa* (Pursh) DC.)
Honeysuckle Family (Caprifoliaceae)

A slender, twining vine, Orange Honeysuckle grows in thickets and woods in the southern part of the province, especially west of the Cascade Mountains. It climbs on shrubs and trees, sometimes up to 6

metres high. The flowers are showy, bright orange and tubular, in dense terminal clusters. The berries are orange to red, juicy and translucent. They are not eaten by any coastal aboriginal groups. The Saanich consider them to be poisonous, although the children liked to suck the nectar from the basal swelling of the flower tube. The Squamish call this plant "swing of the ghosts".

**Twinflower Honeysuckle (*Lonicera involucrata* (Rich.)
Banks ex Spreng.)
Honeysuckle Family (Caprifoliaceae)**

Twinflower Honeysuckle is a bushy shrub, up to 3 metres tall, that grows in damp, open thickets throughout the province, especially along the coast. It is also called Black Twinberry. Its leaves are dark green, paired and elliptical, tapering at both ends. The short tubular flowers, always in twos, are subtended by broad, leafy bracts that are green at first, but later turn deep red. The paired berries are black and shiny. Although reputed to be edible, the berries were not eaten

by any coastal aboriginal groups. The Kwakwaka'wakw believed that if you ate them you would lose your voice. The Nuxalk call them "robin's berries", the Haida call them "Raven's berry" or "Crow's berry" and the Squamish call them "little snake's berry" – only these animals, not people, ate the fruit of this plant.

**Waxberry (*Symphoricarpos albus* (L) Blake)
Honeysuckle Family (Caprifoliaceae)**

Waxberry is a low, bushy shrub, often forming large thickets along roadsides and in clearings and open woods. The paired leaves are bluish-green, rounded and occasionally lobed on young stems. The minute pinkish flowers grow in scattered clusters. The berries are large, soft and white, remaining on the bushes well into winter, when they are especially conspicuous. It is also called Snowberry.

All coastal aboriginal groups believed that Waxberries were poisonous or inedible. A young Saanich girl was said to have died from eating them. The Nuxalk believed they were the Salmonberries of the people in the Land of the Dead. A story was recorded by McIlwraith (1948) of a girl who died, but was brought back to life by shamans. She kept crying for Salmonberries, but since it was mid winter, there

were none. It soon became clear that she wanted Waxberries – they were her Salmonberries. She ate these, but "since there was no food value in them", she died again and this time could not be brought back to life. Waxberries were commonly used medicinally, for sore eyes, or by the Sechelt for removing warts. The Tsimshian regarded them as food for grouse. Among the Washington Salish, only the Squaxin ate them, drying them for winter food.

Yellow Pond-lily (*Nuphar polysepalum* Engelm.)
Water-lily Family (Nymphaeaceae)

Yellow Pond-lily is a perennial aquatic plant with a large horizontal rootstock. The leaves, which float on the surface of lakes and ponds, are round or heart-shaped, like those of ornamental water-lilies, but usually bigger. The solitary flowers are large, yellow and waxy look-ing, with five rounded petals and a large knob at the centre. Yellow Pond-lily is found in ponds, lakes, marshes and muskegs throughout the province.

The seeds were an important food source of the coastal First Peoples of Oregon and California, and the large rootstocks are reported in many edible plants books to be "excellent eating", being rich in starch. But neither seeds nor rootstocks were eaten by the coastal First Peoples of British Columbia, as far as can be determined, although the rootstocks were widely used as medicine for numerous ailments. From personal experience, the roots are extremely bitter and unpleasant, even after prolonged boiling in several changes of water.

Cascara (*Rhamnus purshiana* DC.)
Buckthorn Family (Rhamnaceae)

Cascara is a small alder-like tree, with smooth grey bark and oval leaves, like those of an alder but not coarsely toothed. The flowers are small, greenish and inconspicuous, and the berries are globular, dark and shiny. It commonly grows in sec-ond-growth deciduous woods and thick-ets in the southwestern part of the province, especially southern Vancouver Island, the Gulf Islands and the adjacent mainland. The leaves turn yellow in autumn, but often remain on the trees, ragged and drooping, until mid winter.

Cascara bark is well known as a commercial laxative, and was valued as a tonic and laxative by the coastal First Peoples where it occurred. The berries are edible, but were not eaten by any of the coastal aboriginal groups in British Columbia, although the Makah in Washington apparently ate them fresh in summer. British Columbian groups did not actually consider them poisonous, but rather seemed to ignore them as a food, probably because they were too difficult to collect in quantity. But some aboriginal people believe the fruit to have the same laxative properties as the bark.

Ninebark (*Physocarpus capitatus* (Pursh) Kuntze)
Rose Family (Rosaceae)

A tall, dense shrub of wet bottom lands, Ninebark has noticeably shredding bark and leaves resembling those of High-bush Cranberry or a small maple, with three to five pointed lobes. The flowers are small and white, and grow in rounded clusters, and the fruiting heads are brownish. Ninebark is found along the southern coast of the province, recurring in the interior wet belt. It is generally ignored or casually recognized by most coastal aboriginal groups within its range, but the Nuxalk regard it as a violent poison, in the same league with Devil's Club and Water Hemlock. They use a tea from the inner bark with great caution as an emetic, but believe it to be fatal if prepared improperly.

Ninebark.   Bitter Cherry.

Bitter Cherry (*Prunus emarginata* (Dougl.) Walpers)
Rose Family (Rosaceae)

A shrub or small tree up to 9 metres tall, Bitter Cherry grows in moist second-growth deciduous forests and open woods. It is common throughout the southern part of the province and sporadic along the coast northward, but not on Haida Gwaii. The bark is greyish or reddish, peeling horizontally like birch bark. The leaves are small, oblong, oval and finely toothed. The small, white flowers are in loose clusters, and the cherry-like fruits are bright red and juicy, but extremely bitter. They were not eaten by any of the coastal aboriginal groups of British Columbia, because of their unpleasant taste and difficulty to harvest.

GLOSSARY

Algae (alga, singular) A large group of plants, mostly aquatic or marine, having no true roots, stems, leaves or specialized conduction tissue; includes seaweeds.

Alkaloids A group of complex, basic chemical compounds produced by many types of plants, often severely toxic when ingested by animals. They usually occur in plants as a soluble organic acid-alkaline salt, and are almost always bitter in taste.

Annual A plant that lives only one year or season.

Basal Pertaining to the base or lower part of a plant or structure.

Biennial A plant that lives only two years; flowers and fruits are usually produced only in the second year.

Bifurcated Divided into two parts or branches; forked.

Bract A modified leaf, either small and scale-like or large and petal-like.

Bryophyte Any member of the plant division Bryophyta, comprising the mosses and liverworts.

Bulb A swollen underground bud, composed of a short stem covered with fleshy layers of leaf; e.g., an onion.

Cambium A layer of continuously dividing cells between the wood and the bark of trees and shrubs from which new wood and bark tissues are derived.

Catkin A drooping, elongated cluster of flowers that have no petals, either male or female, as on willows, alders and birches.

Clasping Entwined about or growing very close to something; e.g., the stem of a plant.

Compound Composed of two or more similar parts; e.g., a compound leaf is divided into two or more leaflets with a common leafstalk.

Cone A reproductive structure, either male or female, of certain trees, consisting of a central axis surrounded by numerous woody scales that bear the seeds or pollen; e.g., a pine cone.

Conifer Any cone-bearing tree such as pine, fir or spruce; a major group of gymnosperms.

Corm A fleshy, thickened underground stem at the base of a plant, usually more or less spherical, resembling a bulb, but solid rather than layered.

Crown The leafy or branching head of a tree.

Deciduous Refers to a plant that sheds all its leaves annually, as opposed to being evergreen.

Dicotyledon Any member of a major subgroup of flowering plants (Dicotyledonae), characterized by embryos with two seed-leaves (cotyledons), net-veined leaves and flower parts in fours or fives; as opposed to monocotyledons.

Drupelet One segment of an aggregate fruit such as a raspberry or blackberry.

Elliptical The shape of an ellipse.

Evergreen Refers to a plant having green leaves throughout the year, especially during the winter, as opposed to being deciduous.

Family A category in the classification of plants and animals, ranking above *genus* and below *order*, including two or more related genera. Most family names end in "aced".

Fern Any member of a broad division of non-flowering plants

(Pteridophyta) having true roots, stems, specialized conduction tissue and true leaves, which are usually large and compound or dissected. Reproduction is by spores, usually produced in sori on the lower surfaces or margins of the leaves.

Flowering Plant Any member of a major group of vascular plants, known as angiosperms (Magnoliophyta), characterized by having true flowers and seeds enclosed in a fruit.

Frond The leaf of a fern, often compound or finely dissected.

Fruit A ripened seed-case or ovary and any associated structures that ripen with it.

Fungi (fungus, singular) A broad group of organisms, considered distinct from plants, lacking chlorophyll and true roots, stems and leaves; reproduction is by spores; includes moulds, mildews, rusts, smuts and mushrooms.

Genus (genera, plural) The main subdivision of *family* in the classification of plants and animals, consisting of a group of closely related species. In the scientific name of an organism, the genus name is the first term and the initial letter is always capitalized; e.g., *Acer* is the genus name in *Acer macrophyllum* (Broad-leaved Maple).

Grease A clear oil rendered from a small fish, the Eulachon (Oolichan); used by coastal First Peoples in the same manner as Europeans use butter.

Gymnosperm Any member of a major group of vascular plants (Pinophyta) characterized by having seeds or ovules that are not enclosed in a fruit, but instead are borne in cones or related structures. The conifers are an important subgroup of gymnosperms.

Herbaceous Not woody, having stems that die back to the ground at the end of the growing season.

Holdfast A structure, usually with branching, root-like appendages, by which a seaweed is fastened to the surface it is growing on.

Indusia (indusium, singular) Umbrella-like structures covering the sori of many types of ferns.

Leaflet An ultimate unit of a compound leaf.

Lichen Any member of a large group of composite organisms, each consisting of one or more algae and a fungus growing in a close relationship. Lichens are generally small, forming branching, leafy or encrusting structures on rock, wood and soil.

Lobed Having major divisions extending about halfway to the base or centre; often applied to leaves, such as oak or maple.

Monocotyledon Any member of a major subgroup of flowering plants (Monocotyledonae), having embryos with a single seed-leaf (cotyledon), parallel-veined leaves, and flower parts in threes; as opposed to dicotyledons.

Muskeg A poorly drained area with acid soil conditions, characterized by the presence of Sphagnum moss, Labrador Tea and other specially adapted plants.

Node A joint or portion of a stem from which a leaf or branch has grown.

Opposite In reference to leaves, growing directly across from each other at the same node.

Palmately compound Referring to a compound leaf with the leaflets arising from the same point; e.g., the leaf of a horse-chestnut or lupine.

Perennial A plant that lives more than two years.

Petal Any member of the inside set of floral bracts in flowering plants; usually coloured or white and serving to attract insect or bird pollinators. Many flowers do not have true petals.

Pinna (pinnae, plural) One of the primary lateral divisions of a pinnately compound leaf, such as a fern frond.

Pinnately compound Referring to a compound leaf with leaflets on either side of a central axis in a feather-like arrangement; e.g., the leaf of a walnut or elderberry.

Pinnule An ultimate leaflet of a leaf that is pinnately compound two or more times; i.e., the ultimate division of a compound pinna.

Recurve Curving or curling backward.

Rhizome A creeping underground stem, often fleshy, serving in vegetative reproduction and food storage.

Sepal Any member of the outside set of floral bracts in flowering plants; typically green and leaf-like, but sometimes bright-coloured and petal-like.

Sheath A thin covering surrounding an organ, such as the sheath of a grass leaf surrounding the stem.

Shrub A small woody perennial, usually with several permanent stems instead of a single trunk like that of a tree.

Sorus (sori, plural) A cluster of spore cases on the undersurface of a fern frond.

Species (singular and plural) The fundamental unit in the classification of plants and animals, a subdivision of *genus*, consisting of a group of organisms that have a high degree of similarity, show persistent differences from members of species in the same genus and usually interbreed only among themselves. In a scientific name, the species is designated by the second part, which is not capitalized; e.g. in *Acer macrophyllum* (Broad-leaved Maple), *macrophyllum* is the species designation for the genus *Acer*.

Spike An elongated flower cluster, with flowers attached directly to the central stalk.

Stamen A male or pollen-bearing organ of a flower, consisting of a pollen capsule (anther) and a stalk (filament).

Stipe An erect stem-like portion of a seaweed.

Talus A sloping mass of rock fragments at the base of a mountain or cliff.

Taproot A main root, growing vertically downward, from which smaller branch roots grow out; e.g., a carrot.

Terminal Growing at the end of a stem or branch.

Umbel A flower cluster in which stalks of about the same length grow from a common centre and form a flat or slightly curved surface.

REFERENCES
(1975)

The following annotated list of references was compiled for the first edition of this handbook (1975). It has been updated for this new edition, but is still dated; many of these publications are out of print and can only be found in libraries. More recent references follow under Addition References (1995). This list is organized under three headings: Coastal First Peoples, Plants (botanical information), and Edible, Useful and Poisonous Plants.

Coastal First Peoples of British Columbia and Adjacent Areas

These are only a few of the numerous ethnographic and historical descriptions available. An extensive bibliography can be found in Duff and Kew (1973), listed below. A more recent source is Hoover (1986), listed in Additional References.

Barnett, H.G. 1955. *The Coast Salish of British Columbia.* Eugene, Oregon: University of Oregon Press.

Boas, F. 1921. Ethnology of the Kwakiutl. In *Bureau of American Ethnology, 35th Annual Report*, part 1, 1913-14. Washington, D.C.: Smithsonian Institution, (Out of print, but contains numerous details on the collection, preparation and eating of plant foods by the Kwakwaka'wakw.)

Bouchard, R. 1973. Mainland Comox plant names. Unpublished manuscript written for the British Columbia Indian Language Project, Victoria.

Carlson, R.L., ed. 1970. *Archaeology in British Columbia, New Discoveries. B.C. Studies* 6-7 (Fall-Winter), special issue. (Summarises recent archaeological work in all areas of the province.)

Drucker, P. 1951. *The Northern and Central Nootkan Tribes.* Bureau of American Ethnology, Bulletin 44. Washington, D.C.: Smithsonian Institution. (Some of the information was included in the present handbook.)

Drucker, P. 1955. *Indians of the Northwest Coast.* Garden City, N.Y.: Natural History Press. (Highly recommended as a popular review.)

Drucker, P. 1965. *Cultures of the North Pacific Coast.* San Francisco: Chandler Publishing Company. (Interesting and well worth reading.)

Duff, W. 1952. *The Upper Stalo Indians.* Anthropology in British Columbia Memoir no. 1. Victoria: British Columbia Provincial Museum. (Out of print. Some of the information was included in the present handbook.)

Duff, W. 1964. *The Indian History of British Columbia.* Vol. 1: *The Impact of the White Man.* Anthropology in British Columbia Memoir No. 5. Victoria: British Columbia Provincial Museum. (Contains a wealth of information on B.C. aboriginal groups and their post-contact history.)

Duff, W., and M. Kew. 1973. A select bibliography of anthropology of British Columbia. *B.C. Studies* 19 (Autumn): 73-122. Revised by F. Woodward and Laine Ruus. (Extremely thorough. See also Hoover 1986 in Additional References.)

McIlWraith, T.F. 1948. *The Bella Coola Indians.* Two Volumes. Toronto: University of Toronto Press. (Information on the Nuxalk.)

Sproat, G.M. 1868. *Scenes and Studies of Savage Life.* Reprint 1987. Edited and annotated by Charles Lillard. Victoria: Sono Nis Press. (An early account of observations on Nuu-chah-nulth; some of the information was included in this handbook.)

Suttles, W. 1955. *Katzie Ethnographic Notes.* Anthropology in British Columbia Memoir no. 2. Victoria: British Columbia Provincial Museum. (Some of the information was included in this handbook.)

Swanton, J. 1905. Contributions to the Ethnology of the Haida. American Museum of Natural History, Memoir No. 8, Part 1; Jesup North Pacific Expedition, Vol. 5, Pt. 1.

Plants in British Columbia

Calder, J.A., and R.L. Taylor. 1968. *Flora of the Queen Charlotte Islands,* Part 1. Monograph no. 4. Ottawa: Canada Department of Agriculture, Research Branch. (A detailed, but technical description of plants on Haida Gwaii.)

Clark, L.J. 1973. *Wild Flowers of British Columbia.* Sidney, B.C.: Gray's Publishing. (A beautifully illustrated account of B.C. flowers and berries.)

Eastham, J. W. 1947. Supplement to *Flora of Southern British Columbia* by J.K. Henry. Special Publication no. 1. Victoria: British Columbia Provincial Museum. (Updates Henry's *Flora*; technical.)

Garman, E.H. 1963. *Pocket Guide to Trees and Shrubs in British Columbia.* Handbook no. 31. Victoria: British Columbia Provincial Museum. (Comprehensive and concise, with illustrations for many species.)

Haskin, L. 1934. *Wild Flowers of the Pacific Coast.* Portland: Binfords & Mort. (Very interesting, with many details on First Peoples' uses of plants, botanical descriptions and photographs of most species; out of print.)

Henry, J.K. 1915. *Flora of Southern British Columbia and Vancouver Island.* Toronto: W.J. Gage & Co. (Detailed, but outdated; technical and unillustrated.)

Hitchcock, C.L., A. Cronquist, M. Owenby and J.W. Thompson. 1955-1969. *Vascular Plants of the Pacific Northwest,* Parts 1-5. Seattle: University of Washington Press. (An extremely comprehensive, well-illustrated series, covering at least the southern part of British Columbia; an excellent reference work, available in most libraries; also recently published in an abridged field edition, which is rather technical for beginners.)

Krajina, V.J. 1969. Ecology of forest trees in British Columbia. *Ecology of Western North America* 2 (1). (Technical, but extremely comprehensive; contains a description of the biogeoclimatic zones of the province.)

Lyons, C.P. 1952 (Revised in 1 965). *Trees, Shrubs and Flowers to Know in British Columbia.* Vancouver: J.M. Dent & Sons (Canada). (Popularly written; excellent for the beginner, with nontechnical descriptions and line drawings of most common vascular plants in B.C.)

Scagel, R.F. 1967. *Guide to Common Seaweeds of British Columbia.* Handbook no. 27. Victoria: British Columbia Provincial Museum. (Slightly technical, but well illustrated and thorough, with a good introduction; out of print.)

Szczawinski, A.F. 1962. *The Heather Family of British Columbia.* Handbook no. 19. Victoria: British Columbia Provincial Museum. (Excellent reference book for this family; contains line illustrations and distribution maps.)

Taylor, T.M.C. 1956. *The Ferns and Fern-allies of British Columbia.* Handbook no. 12. Victoria: British Columbia Provincial Museum. (Excellent reference book with illustrations.)

Taylor, T.M.C. 1966. *The Lily Family of British Columbia.* Handbook no. 25. Victoria: British Columbia Provincial Museum. (Excellent reference book with illustrations.)

Taylor, T.M.C. 1973. *The Rose Family of British Columbia.* Handbook no. 30. Victoria: British Columbia Provincial Museum. (Slightly technical; lacks common names, but illustrated, with distribution maps.)

Edible, Useful and Poisonous Plants of Coastal British Columbia and Adjacent Areas

Anderson, J.R. 1925. *Trees and Shrubs, Food, Medicinal, and Poisonous Plants of British Columbia.* Victoria: King's Printers. (Out of print, but obtainable at many libraries; contains much useful and original information.)

French, D.H. 1965. Ethnobotany of the Pacific Northwest Indians. *Economic Botany* 19 (4): 378-382. (Very general; mostly applicable to American aboriginal groups.)

Gunther, E. 1945 (revised in 1973). *Ethnobotany of Western Washington.*

Publications in Anthropology 10 (1). Seattle: University of Washington Press. (Extremely detailed for Western Washington groups; contains original information; revised edition illustrated.)

Kingsbury, J. M. 1964. *Poisonous Plants of the United States and Canada.* Englewood Cliffs, N.J.: Prentice-Hall. (A rather technical but highly informative account of poisonous plants and their products, especially in relation to livestock poisoning.)

Kirk, D.R. 1970. *Wild Edible Plants of the Western United States.* Healdsburg, Ca: Naturegraph Publishers. (Includes many plants of the British Columbia coast, with botanical descriptions and illustrations.)

Smith, H.I. 1928. Materia medica of the Bella Coola and neighbouring tribes of British Columbia. National Museum of Canada, Bulletin no. 56: pp. 47-68. (Restricted to medicinal plants, but very interesting.)

Sweet, M. 1962. *Common Edible and Useful Plants of the West.* Healdsburg, Ca: Naturegraph Publishers. (Illustrated; includes a number of plants of the British Columbia coast.)

Steedman, E.V. 1929. The ethnobotany of the Thompson Indians of British Columbia. In *Bureau of American Ethnology, 45th Annual Report, 1927-28.* Washington, D.C.: Smithsonian Institution. (Contains a section on edible plants; not illustrated.)

Szczawinski, A.F., and G.A.Hardy. 1971. *Guide to Common Edible Plants of British Columbia.* Handbook no. 20. Victoria: British Columbia Provincial Museum. (An excellent general reference; well illustrated.)

Turner, N. 1973. The ethnobotany of the Bella Coola Indians of British Columbia. *Syesis,* vol 6: 193-220.

Turner, N., and M.A.M. Bell. 1971. The ethnobotany of the Coast Salish Indians of Vancouver Island. *Economic Botany* 25 (1): 63-104.

Turner, N., and M.A.M. Bell. 1973. The ethnobotany of the Southern Kwakiutl Indians of British Columbia. *Economic Botany* 27 (3): 257-310.

Turner, N., and R.L. Taylor. 1972. A review of the northwest coast tobacco mystery. *Syesis,* vol. 5: 249-257. (A discussion of the tobacco cultivated by the Haida and Tlingit.)

Underhill, J.E. 1974. *Wild Berries of the Pacific Northwest.* Saanichton, B.C.: Hancock House Publishers. (An interesting and informative guide to wild fruits; well illustrated; contains recipes.)

ADDITIONAL REFERENCES

Since this handbook was first released in 1975, research on aboriginal culture and traditional food plants in British Columbia has continued. Many books and articles have been published on these topics; some relevant publications are listed here. A major project undertaken by the Nuxalk Nation, with nutritionist Harriet V. Kuhnlein and other colleagues, was the Nuxalk Food and Nutrition Project, described in a series of publications authored or co-authored by Dr Kuhnlein and detailed in Kuhnlein and Turner (1991).

Compton, Brian D. 1993. Upper North Wakashan and Southern Tsimshian ethnobotany: the knowledge and usage of plants and fungi among the Oweekeno, Hanaksiala (Kitlope and Kemano), Haisla (Kitamaat) and Kitasoo peoples of the central and north coasts of British Columbia. Ph.D. diss., Department of Botany, University of British Columbia, Vancouver.

Compton, Brian D. 1993. The North Wakashan "wild carrots" clarification of some ethnobotanical ambiguity in Pacific Northwest Apiaceae. *Economic Botany* 47 (3): 297-303.

Compton, Brian D. 1995. "Ghost's Ears" (*Exobasidium* sp. affin. *vaccinii*) and Fool's Huckleberries (*Menziesia ferruginea* Smith): a unique report of mycophagy on the central coast of British Columbia. *Journal of Ethnobiology* 15 (1): 89-98.

Fladmark, Knut R. 1986. *British Columbia Prehistory.* Ottawa: National Museum of Man, National Museums of Canada.

Gottesfeld, Leslie M. Johnson. 1992. The importance of bark products in the aboriginal economies of northwestern British Columbia, Canada. *Economic Botany* 46 (2): 148-157.

Gottesfeld, Leslie M. Johnson. 1994. Aboriginal burning for vegetation management in northwest British Columbia. *Human Ecology* 22 (2): 171-188.

Hoover, Alan L. 1986. A selection of publications on the Indians of British Columbia. Unpublished bibliography. Royal British Columbia Museum Library. (An update of Duff and Kew, 1973.)

Keely, Patrick B. 1980. Nutrient composition of selected important plant foods of the pre-contact diet of the northwest Native American people. Master's Thesis, University of Washington, Seattle.

Kirk, Ruth. 1986. *Wisdom of the Elders: Native Traditions on the Northwest Coast.* Vancouver: Douglas and McIntyre (in association with the Royal British Columbia Museum, Victoria).

Kruckeberg, Arthur R. 1982. *Gardening with Native Plants of the Pacific Northwest.* Vancouver: Douglas & McIntyre.

'Ksan, People of. 1980. *Gathering What the Great Nature Provided. Food Traditions of the Gitksan.* Vancouver: Douglas & McIntyre; Seattle: University of Washington Press.

Kuhnlein, H.V. 1984. Traditional and contemporary Nuxalk foods. *Nutrition Research* 4 (5): 789-809.

Kuhnlein, Harriet V., and Nancy J. Turner. 1987. Cow Parsnip (*Heracleum lanatum* Michx.): an indigenous vegetable of native people of northwestern North America. *Journal of Ethnobiology* 6(2):309-324.

Kuhnlein, Harriet V., and Nancy J. Turner. 1991. *Traditional Plant Foods of Canadian Indigenous Peoples. Nutrition, Botany and Use.* Food and Nutrition in History and Anthropology, edited by Solomon Katz, vol. 8. Philadelphia: Gordon and Breach Science Publishers. (Contains nutrient tables and many other references for food plants.)

Kuhnlein, Harriet V., Nancy J. Turner and Paul D. Kluckner. 1982. Nutritional significance of two important root foods (Springbank Clover and Pacific Silverweed) use by native people of the coast of British Columbia. *Ecology of Food and Nutrition* 12: 89-95.

Laforet, Andrea, Nancy J. Turner and Annie York. 1993. Traditional Foods of the Fraser Canyon Nlaka'pamux. pp. 191-214. In *American Indian Linguistics and Ethnography in Honor of Laurence C. Thompson,* edited by Anthony Mattina and Timothy Montler. University of Montana Occasional Papers in Linguistics no. 10. Missoula: University of Montana Press.

Lepofsky, D.L., N.J. Turner and H.V. Kuhnlein. 1984. Determining the availability of traditional wild plant foods: an example of Nuxalk foods, Bella Coola, British Columbia. *Ecology of Food and Nutrition* 16: 223-41.

McMillan, Alan D. 1988. *Native Peoples and Cultures of Canada: An Anthropological Overview.* Vancouver: Douglas & McIntyre.

Meidinger, Del and Jim Pojar, eds. 1991. *Ecosystems of British Columbia.* Victoria: Ministry of Forests.

Morrison, R.B., and C. R. Wilson, eds. 1986. *Native Peoples: The Canadian Experience.* Toronto: McClelland and Stewart.

Norton, H.H. 1979a. Evidence for Bracken Fern as a food for aboriginal peoples of western Washington. *Economic Botany* 33: 384-396.

Norton, H.H. 1979b. The association between anthropogenic prairies and important food plants in western Washington.

Northwest Anthropological Research Notes 13: 175-200.

Norton, H.H. 1981. Plant use in Kaigani Haida culture: correction of an ethnohistorical oversight. *Economic Botany* 35: 434-449.

Norton, H.H., E.S. Hunn, C.S. Martinsen and P.B. Keely. 1984. Vegetable food products of the foraging economies of the Pacific Northwest. *Ecology of Food and Nutrition* 14: 219-228.

Nuxalk Food and Nutrition Program. 1984. *Nuxalk Food and Nutrition Handbook*. Bella Coola, B.C.: Nuxalk Food and Nutrition Program and Nuxalk Nation Council.

Pojar, Jim and Andy MacKinnon, eds. 1994. *Plants of Coastal British Columbia including Washington, Oregon & Alaska*. Edmonton: Lone Pine Publishing.

Suttles, Wayne. 1987. *Coast Salish Essays*. Vancouver: Talonbooks; Seattle: University of Washington Press.

Suttles, Wayne, ed. 1990. *Northwest Coast*. Handbook of North American Indians, edited by William C. Sturtevant, vol 7. Washington D.C.: Smithsonian Institution.

Szczawinski, Adam F., and Nancy J. Turner. 1978. *Edible Garden Weeds of Canada*. Edible Wild Plants of Canada, no. 1. Toronto: Fitzhenry and Whiteside. (Originally published by National Museum of Natural Sciences, Ottawa.)

Szczawinski, Adam F., and Nancy J. Turner. 1980. *Wild Green Vegetables of Canada*. Edible Wild Plants of Canada, no. 4. Toronto: Fitzhenry and Whiteside. (Originally published by National Museum of Natural Sciences, Ottawa.)

Turner, Nancy J. 1978. *Food Plants of British Columbia Indians*. Part 2: *Interior Peoples*. Handbook no. 36. Victoria: British Columbia Provincial Museum.

Turner, Nancy J. 1979. *Plants in British Columbia Indian Technology*. Handbook no. 38. Victoria: British Columbia Provincial Museum.

Turner, Nancy J. 1981a. A gift for the taking: the untapped potential of some food plants of North American Native peoples. *Canadian Journal of Botany* 59(11): 2331-2357.

Turner, Nancy J. 1981b. Indian use of *Shepherdia canadensis*, Soapberry, in western North America. *Davidsonia* 12(1):1-14.

Turner, Nancy J. 1991a. Wild berries. In *Berries*, edited by Jennifer Bennett, pp. 49-69. Toronto: Harrowsmith Books.

Turner, Nancy J. 1991b. Burning mountain sides for better crops: aboriginal landscape burning in British Columbia. *Archaeology in Montana* 32 (2), special issue. (Excerpts reprinted in *International Journal of Ecoforestry* 10(3):116-122, 1994.)

Turner, Nancy J. 1992. Plant resources of the Stl'atl'imx (Fraser River Lillooet) people: a window into the past. In *Complex Cultures of the British Columbia Plateau: Traditional Stl'atl'imx Resource Use*, edited by Brian

Hayden, pp. 405-469. Vancouver: University of British Columbia Press.

Turner, Nancy J., Randy Bouchard and Dorothy I.D. Kennedy. 1981. *Ethnobotany of the Okanagan-Colville Indians of British Columbia and Washington.* Occasional Paper no. 21. Victoria: British Columbia Provincial Museum.

Turner, Nancy J., and Alison Davis. 1993. When everything was scarce: the role of plants as famine foods in northwestern North America. *Journal of Ethnobiology* 13(2): 1-28.

Turner, N.J., and B.S. Efrat. 1982. *Ethnobotany of the Hesquiat Indians of Vancouver Island.* Cultural Recovery Paper no. 2. Victoria: British Columbia Provincial Museum.

Turner, Nancy J., Leslie M.J. Gottesfeld, Harriet V. Kuhnlein and Adolf Ceska. 1992. Edible Wood Fern rootstocks of western North America: solving an ethnobotanical puzzle. *Journal of Ethnobiology* 12(1):1-34.

Turner, Nancy J., and Harriet V. Kuhnlein. 1982. Two important "root" foods of the northwest coast Indians: Springbank Clover (*Trifolium wormskioldii*) and Pacific Silverweed (*Potentilla anserina* ssp. *pacifica*). *Economic Botany* 36(4):411-432.

Turner, Nancy J., and Harriet V. Kuhnlein. 1983. Camas (*Camassia* spp.) and Rice Root (*Fritillaria* spp.): two liliaceous "root" foods of the northwest coast Indians. *Ecology of Food and Nutrition* 13:199-219.

Turner, Nancy J., Harriet V. Kuhnlein and Keith N. Egger. 1985. The Cottonwood Mushroom (*Tricholoma populinum* Lange): a food resource of the interior Salish Indian peoples of British Columbia. *Canadian Journal of Botany* 65:921-927.

Turner, Nancy J., and Adam F. Szczawinski. 1978. *Wild Coffee and Tea Substitutes of Canada.* Edible Wild Plants of Canada no. 2. Toronto: Fitzhenry and Whiteside. (Originally published by National Museum of Natural Sciences, Ottawa.)

Turner, Nancy J., and Adam F. Szczawinski. 1979. *Edible Wild Fruits and Nuts of Canada.* Edible Wild Plants of Canada no. 3. Toronto: Fitzhenry and Whiteside (Originally published by National Museum of Natural Sciences, Ottawa.)

Turner, Nancy J., and Adam F. Szczawinski. 1991. *Common Poisonous Plants and Mushrooms of North America.* Portland: Timber Press.

Turner, Nancy J., John Thomas, Barry F. Carlson and Robert T. Ogilvie. 1983. *Ethnobotany of the Nitinaht Indians of Vancouver Island.* Occasional Paper no. 24. Victoria: British Columbia Provincial Museum.

Turner, Nancy J., Laurence C. Thompson, M. Terry Thompson and Annie Z. York. 1990. *Thompson Ethnobotany: Knowledge and Usage of Plants by the Thompson Indians of British Columbia.* Memoir No. 3. Victoria: Royal British Columbia Museum.

Wells, N. Oliver. 1987. *The Chilliwacks and Their Neighbors.* Vancouver: Talonbooks.

INDEX

Acer macrophyllum 55
Alder, Red 6, 38, 43, **64-65**
    Oregon 64
Allium acuminatum 40
    cepa 133
    cernuum 40
    species 40
Alnus rubra 6, 64
Amelanchier alnifolia 110
    florida 110
apples (cultivated) **135**
Aralia nudicaulis 61
Arbutus 43
Arctostaphylos uva-ursi 76
Arrow-grass **39-40**
Arrow-head 36
Arrow-leaf 36
Artichoke, Jerusalem 43
Arum, Yellow 37
Ash, Sitka Mountain **129**
Athyrium filix-femina 25
Avalanche Lily, Yellow 45

Baked-apple 121
Balsamorhiza sagittata 43
Barberry 63
beans (cultivated) **134**
Bearberry 76
Berberis aquifolium 63
    nervosa 63
Bilberry, Bog **89**
    Mountain **82**
    Oval-leaved 84
    Red 87
Bird-cherry 114
Black Haw 111
Black Hawthorn **111**

Black Raspberry 123
blackberries (cultivated) **135**
Blackberry, Pacific 127
    Trailing Wild 113, **127-28**
Blackcap 16, **123**
Blechnum spicant 29
blueberries (generic) 16, 18, 84
Blueberry, Alaska 6, **81**, 84
    Bog 83, 89
    Canada **83-84**, 89
    Grey 84
    Mouldy 84
    Oval-leaved 6, 81, **84**
    Sour-top 83
    Velvet-leaf 83
Boschniakia hookeri 107
Brassica rapa 134
Brodiaea hyacinthina 41
Buffalo-berry, Russet 73
Bunchberry 6, 16, **71**

Calypso 2, **52-53**
Calypso bulbosa 52
Camas, Blue vii, x, 6, 9, 13, 16, 18, **42-**
    44, 46, 48, 65, 74, 94, 139
    Common 42
    Death 2, 41, 42, 44, **139-40**
    Edible 42
    Sweet 42
    White 140
Camassia leichtlinii 42
    quamash 42
Caraway, Wild **59-60**, 132
Carrot, Indian xi, 56
    Wild 16, 56, 60, 132
carrots (cultivated) 10, 57, **133**
Cascara **143-44**

Cat-tail 43
cedar, Western Red- 6, 7, 14, 15, 15, 20,
    21, 34, 44, 46, 68, 69, 74, 78,
    80, 88, 93, 95, 98, 112, 115,
    116, 118, 125
    Yellow- 6, 7
cherries (cultivated) **135**
Cherry, Bitter **145**
Cicuta douglasii 59, 61, 140
Cinquefoil, Pacific 13, 16, 17, 94, 109,
    115-16
Cirsium arvense 62
    brevistylum 62
    edule 62
    vulgare 62
Citrus sinensis 135
Clintonia uniflora 138
Cloudberry **121-22**
Clover, Perennial 94
    Springbank 13, 16, 17, **94-95**, 116
    Wild 94
Cobnut 65
Conioselinum pacificum 56
Conium maculatum 59
Cornus canadensis 71
    unalaschkensis 71
Corylus cornuta 65
Cottonwood, Black 2, 10, 14, 16, 130
Crabapple, Oregon 117
    Pacific 117
    Western 117
    Wild 16, **117-18**
crabapples (generic) 16, 18, 50
Cranberry, Bog 18, **86-87**, 90, 126
    High-bush 6, 18, 32, 35, 51, **69-
    70**, 118, 140, 144
    Low-bush **90**
    Moss 86
    Mountain 90
    Rock 90
    Wild 86
cranberries (generic) 16, 87, 90
Crataegus douglasii 111
Crowberry **75**
Currant, Blue 98
    Prickly 100
    Red-flowering x, 6, **103**
    Skunk 98
    Stink 38, **98-99**
    Swamp 100
    Trailing 101
    White-flowered **101-102**

Wild Black 101
currants (cultivated) 78, **134**
    (generic) 16, 88

Daucus carota 57, 133
    pusillus 57
Devil's Club 101, **141**
Dock, Western 108, 134
    Yellow 108
Dogwood, Dwarf 71
Dryopteris austriaca 26
    expansa 26
    filix-mas 26

Easter Lily 45
Easter Lily, Pink 44
Eelgrass 20, **53-54**, 57
Egregia menziesii 20
elderberries (generic) 11, 16, 17, 68
Elderberry, Blue 6, **66-67**, 67
    Red **67-68**, 78, 84
Empetrum nigrum 75
Epilobium angustifolium 106
    latifolium 107
Equisetum arvense 23
    maximum 23
    telmateia 23
Erythronium grandiflorum 45
    oregonum 45
    revolutum 44
Eulachon 10, 16, 18, 93, 136
Eulachon fat 88
    grease – see Grease

False Hellebore 139
False Lady's Slipper 52
False Solomon's Seal 51
Fern, Bracken 24, **30-31**, 38, 92, 116
    Deer 29
    Lady **25**
    Licorice 11, **27-28**, 79
    Male 26, 27
    Polypody 27
    Spiny Wood 25, **26-27**, 28, 29
    Sword **29**
ferns (generic) 14, 15, 16, 41, 43, 57, 69,
    116, 147
Filbert, Wild 65
Fireweed 10, 16, **106-107**
Foxberry 121
Fragaria chiloensis 112
    spp. (cultivated) 135

vesca 112
virginiana 112
Fritillaria camschatcensis 46
  lanceolata 47

Gairdner's Yampah 59
Gaultheria shallon 77
Ginseng, Wild 61
Glaux maritima ssp. *obtusifolia* 109
gooseberries (cultivated) **134**
  (generic) 16, 76, 122
Gooseberry, Coastal Black **99-100**
  Gummy 102
  Red-flowered 102
  Sticky 6, **102-103**
  Swamp 100
Goose-tongue, 72
Grease (Eulachon oil) 10, 11, 14, 16, 18,
  20, 22, 26, 27, 29, 30, 35, 45,
  46, 47, 51, 54, 57, 58, 68, 70,
  76, 78, 88, 91, 93, 95, 98, 99,
  100, 108, 110, 112, 115, 118,
  127, 130, 136, 148
Greyberry 98
Ground Cone **107-108**

Hawthorn, Black **111-12**
Hazelnut 16, **65-66**
Helianthus tuberosus 43
Hellebore, Green 139
  False 139
  Indian 2, **139**, 140
Hemlock, Mountain 5, 6, 33
  Poison 59
  Water 2, 59, 61, **140-41**, 144
  Western viii, 2, 5, 6, 10, 16, 20,
  27, **33-35**, 54, 74, 130
Hemlock-parsley, Pacific xi, **56-57**, 60,
  133
Heracleum lanatum 58
Honeysuckle, Orange **141**
  Twinflower **142**
Horsetail, Common **23-24**
  Giant **23-24**
Huckleberry, Black 82
  Black Mountain 82
  Black Winter 85
  Bog 89
  Cascade 82
  Evergreen x, xii, 16, 64, **85**
  Red 68, **87-88**, 134
  Shot 85

Twin-leaved 82
Indian Carrot xi, 56
  Celery 58
  Hellebore 2, **139**, 140
  ice-cream vi, 10, 11, 73-74
  Plum 17, **114-15**
  Rhubarb 58, 109
  Rice 6, 16, 46, 47, 132
  Spinach 131
  Swamp Potato 36
  Thistle **63-64**
  wax paper 38

June Berry 110
Kalmia microphylla 80
Kelp, Boa 20
  Giant **19-20**, 33
Kinnikinnick x, 16, **76-77**, 107, 137

Labrador Tea vii, 11, 28, **79-80**
Labrador Tea, Glandular 80
Laurel, Swamp 80
Laver, Red **21-22**
Ledum glandulosum 80
  groenlandicum 79
  palustre ssp. *groenlandicum* 79
Licorice, Chinook 91
Lilium columbianum 49
  parviflorum 49
Lily, Black 46
  Chocolate 2, 6, 16, 46, **47-48**
  Columbia 49
  Easter 45
  Pink Easter 44
  Pink Fawn **44-45**
  Tiger 2, **49**
  Yellow Pond- **143**
Lily-of-the-valley, Wild **50-51**, 52, 138
Lingon Berry 90
Lomatium utriculatum 57
Lonicera ciliosa 141
  involucrata 142
Lupine, Beach 91
  Blue **92-93**
  Nootka 92
  Seashore **91-92**, 93
lupines (generic) 2, 16, 51, 93
Lupinus littoralis 91
  nootkatensis 92
Lysichiton americanus 37

Macrocystis integrifolia 19

Mahonia 63
Mahonia aquifolium 63
    nervosa 63
Mahonia, Tall 63
Maianthemum canadense 50
    dilatatum 50
Malus fusca 117
    spp. 135
Malt-berry 121
Maple, Big-leaf 55
    Broad-leaved 6, **55-56**
    Common 55
Mare's tail 23
Mars apple 121
Micromeria douglasii 104
Milkwort, Sea 2, 16, **109-110**, 116
Mission Bells 46
Mountain Ash, Sitka **129**

Nettle, Northwest 131
    Purple Hedge **105**
    Stinging 105, **131**
nettles (generic) 16
Nicotiana quadrivalvis 136
    ssp. 136
    tabacum 136
Ninebark **144**
Nuphar polysepalum 143
Nuttallia cerasiformis 114

Oak, Garry 6, **97**
Oemlaria cerasiformis 114
Onion, Fool's 41
    Hooker's **40-41**
    Nodding **40-41**
    Poison 41, 140
onions (cultivated) **133**
    wild vii, x, 16, **40-41**, 133
Oolichan – see Eulachon
Oplopanax horridus 141
oranges **135**
Oregon Crabapple 177
Oregon Grape **63-64**, 102
Oregon Grape, Dull-leaved 63
    Tall 63
Oryza sativa 133
Osmaronia cerasiformis 114
Oso-berry 114
Oxycoccus microcarpus 86
    palustris 86

Parsnip, Cow 10, 16, 56, **58-59**, 134, 140, 141
    Water **60-61**
parsnips (cultivated) **133**
Pastinaca sativa 133
peaches **135**
pears **135**
peas **134**
Perideridia gairdneri 59
Phaseolus vulgaris 134
Phyllospadix scouleri 54
    torreyi 54
Physocarpus capitatus 144
Picea sitchensis 32
Pigeonberry 71
Pine, Lodgepole 6, 35
Pink Slipper-orchid 52
Pinus contorta 6, 35
Pisum sativum 134
Plantago maritima 39
Plantain, Seaside 39
Plum, Indian 17, **114-15**
plums (cultivated) **135**
Poison Hemlock 59
Polypodium glycyrrhiza 27
    vulgare var. *occidentale* 28
    hesperium 28
Polystichum munitum 29
Pond-lily, Yellow **143**
Populus trichocarpa 130
Poque 107
Porphyra abbottae 21
    perforata 21
    pseudolanceolata 22
    torta 22
Potato, Indian Swamp 36
potatoes (cultivated) 2, 10, 18, 36, 134, **135-136**
Potentilla anserina 115
    anserina ssp. *pacifica* 115
    pacifica 115
Prunus emarginata 145
    spp. (cultivated) 135
Pteridium aquilinum 30
Pyrus diversifolia 117
    fusca 117
    spp. (cultivated) 135

Queenscup **138**
Quercus garryana 97

raspberries (cultivated)   122, **135**
    wild (generic)   16
Raspberry, Black   123
    Trailing Wild   **125-26**
    Wild   122, 123, 125
Rhamnus purshiana   143
Rheum hybridum   134
rhubarb (cultivated)   **134**
Rhubarb, Indian   108
Ribes bracteosum   98
    divaricatum   99
    lacustre   100
    laxiflorum   101
    lobbii   102
    sanguineum   103
    spp. (cultivated)   134
rice   10, 17, **133**
Rice, Indian   6, 16, 46, 47, 133
Rice Root   6, 17, **46-47**, 47, 53, 133
River-beauty   107
Rorippa nasturtium-acquaticum   134
Rosa gymnocarpa   119
    nutkana   119
    pisocarpa   119
Rose, Common Wild   **119-20**
    Dwarf Wild   **119-20**
    Nootka   119
    Swamp   **119-20**
roses, wild   16, **119-20**
Rubus chamaemorus   121
Rubus idaeus   122
    leucodermis   123
    parviflorus   124
    pedatus   125
    spp. (cultivated)   135
    spectabilis   126
    ursinus   127
Rumex acetosella   135
    occidentalis   108

Sagittaria cuneata   36
    latifolia   36
Salal   x, 10, 14, 16, 17, 42, 51, 64, 68, 71,
    74, **77-78**, 81, 84, 98, 107, 111,
    117, 118, 124
Salmonberry   10, 13, 16, 17, 68, 93, 95,
    126-27, 142
Salmonberry, Ground   128
Salt-grass   39
Sambucus cerulea   66
    glauca   66

pubens   67
racemosa   67
Sarsaparilla   **61-62**
Saskatoon Berry   10, 16, 18, 89, 110
Satureja douglasii   104
Scouring Rush   23
Sea-grass   54
Sedum   72
Sedum divergens   72
    integrifolium   72
    oreganum   72
    spathulifolium   72
Service Berry   110
Shad-bush   110
Sheep Sorrel   135
Shepherdia canadensis   73
Silverweed, Pacific   115
Sium suave   60
Skunk Bush   114
Skunk Cabbage   12, 14, 25, 34, **37-39**,
    68, 69, 78, 88, 91, 95, 98
Smilacina racemosa   51
    stellata   51
Snowberry   142
Soapberry   vii, 10, 16, 18, 43, **73-74**
Solanum tuberosum   135
Solomon's Seal, False   **51-52**
    Star-flowered   **51-52**
    Two-leaved   50
Soopolallie   73
Sorbus occidentalis   129
    sitchensis   129
Sour-grass   **135**
Spring Gold   57
Spruce, Sitka   2, 6, 14, 20, **32-33**
Squashberry   69
Stachys ciliata   105
    cooleyae   105
Stonecrop   **72**
strawberries (cultivated)   134, 135
    wild   x, 16, **113**
Strawberry, Blue-leaf   **113**
    Crow's   72
    Seaside   **113**
    Tall   **113**
Streptopus amplexifolius   138
Sunflower, Spring   43
Surf-grass   54
Sweet-berry   89
Symphoricarpos albus, 241
Symplocarpus foetidus   38

Tea, Glandular Labrador 80
  Haida 79
  Hudson's Bay 79
  Labrador vii, 11, 28, **79-80**
  Swamp 79
  Trapper's 80
Thimbleberry 16, 74, 113, **124-25**, 126, 127
Thistle, Canada 62
  Edible 62
  Indian **62-63**
  Scottish 62
Thornberry 111
Thuja plicata 6
tobacco 18, 76, 77, **136-37**
Trifolium wormskjoldii 94
Triglochin maritimum 39
Tsuga heterophylla 33
  mertensiana 33
turnips 3, 10, 18, **134**
Twinberry, Black 142
Twisted Stalk **138**
Typha latifolia 43

Urtica dioica 131
  lyallii 131

Vaccinium alaskense 81
  caespitosum 82
  canadense 83
  deliciosum 82
  membranaceum 82
  myrtilloides 83
  ovalifolium 84
  ovatum 83
  oxycoccus 86
  parvifolium 87
  uliginosum 83, 89
  vitis-idaea ssp. *minus* 90
Veratrum viride 139
Vetch, Giant **96**
Viburnum edule 69
Vicia gigantea 96
Violet, Yellow Dog-tooth 2

Wapato **36-37**
Watercress **134**
Waxberry **142-43**
Whortleberry 89
Willow Herb 106
Yerba Buena **104**
Zigadenus venenosus 41, 44, 139
Zostera marina 53

The photographs in this book, other than those by R.D. and N.J. Turner, are by:
Harold Hosford, RBCM – pp. 20, 21, 22, 23, 25, 28, 29, 30, 32, 33, 40(right), 41(lower), 42, 46, 47(lower), 48, 49(upper), 49(lower), 52, 53, 55, 58, 59, 119 and 120. © 1975 Royal British Columbia Museum.
E.S. Curtis – back cover, and pp. xii, 12, 13(left) and 18.
W. van Dieren – pp. 51(right), 111 and 114. © 1995 Royal B.C. Museum.
Robert A. Cannings, RBCM – pp. 92 and 121. © 1975, 1995 R.A. Cannings.
Andrew Niemann, RBCM – pp. 13(right) and 15. © 1995 Royal B.C. Museum.
A. Bernand – p. 102. © 1975 A. Bernand.
T.C. Brayshaw – p. 44. © 1995 T.C. Brayshaw.

The author and publishers thank A. Bernand, T.C. Brayshaw, Robert A. Cannings and W. van Dieren for permission to reproduce their photographs in this book.

Cover design by Chris Tyrrell, RBCM.
Map on page 8 drawn by Gerald Luxton, RBCM. © Royal B.C. Museum.